Séance of the Bees

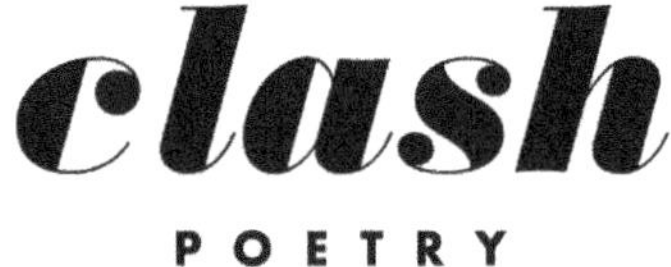

clash
POETRY

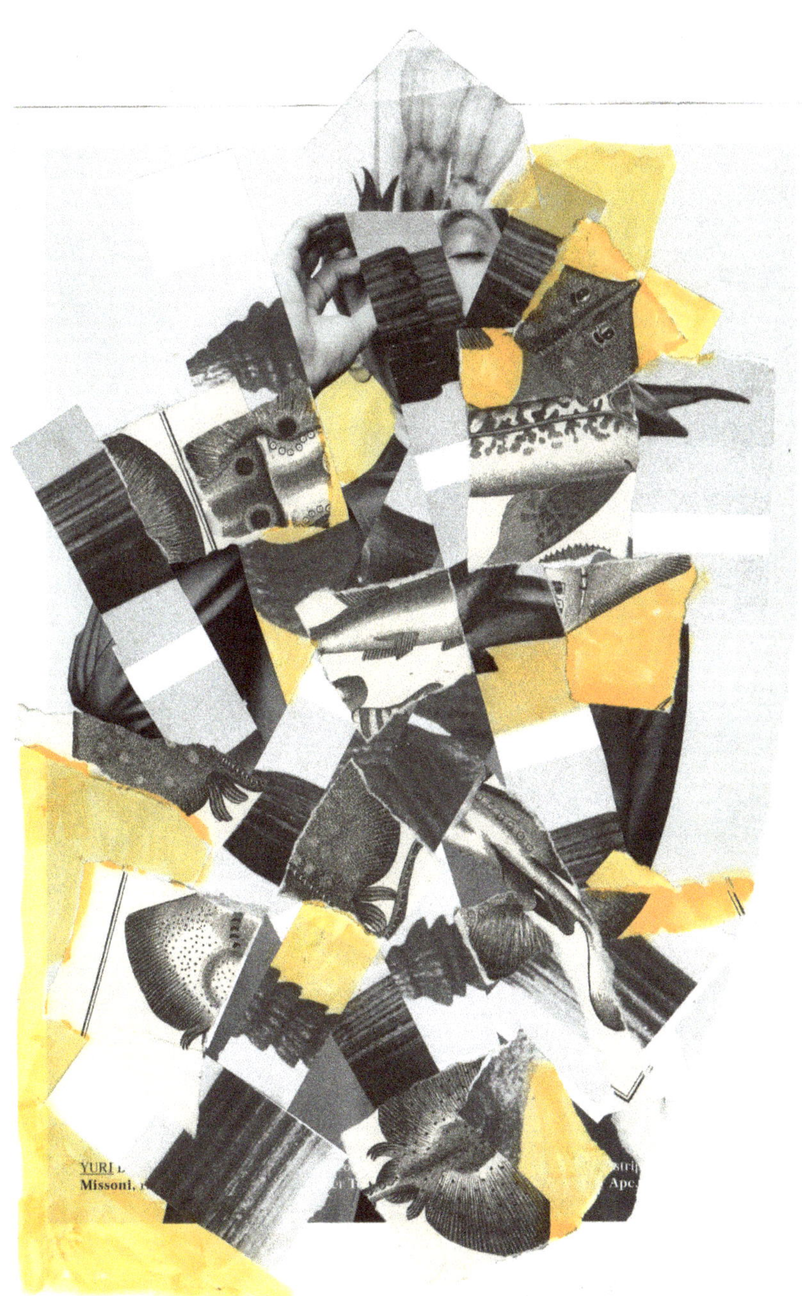

YURI
Missoni,
stri
Ape

Séance of the Bees

Cover: Séance of the Bees, 2016

Alien Plant Lady, 2019

Becoming Swarm
        Séance of the Bees, 2018
        Planchette
        Butterfly Lady I, 2017
        She Who Hems from Source
        Channel
        Breathe as Passage
        Sisters, 2017

Structure of a Flower
        Botanical Lady I, 2017
        The Way the Language Was
        Snake Lady, 2017
        The Structure of a Flower: Stigma
        Plant Birds, 2017
        The Way the Language Was
        Serpens American, 2023
        The Structure of a Flower: Sepal
        Walking Ensemble, 2017
        Afterworld
        Lady Death, 2020

Hive Song
        Swarm / An Arm
        Metaphysical Final Girl, 2019
        Catacombs
        Flight Pattern
        Lady of the Horns, 2017

The Bees
        O'Hara
        Dickinson
        Vicuña
        Stevens
        Spicer
        Dickinson

Séance of the Bees

Andrea Rexilius

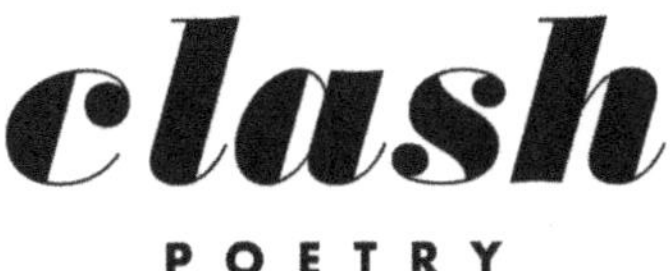

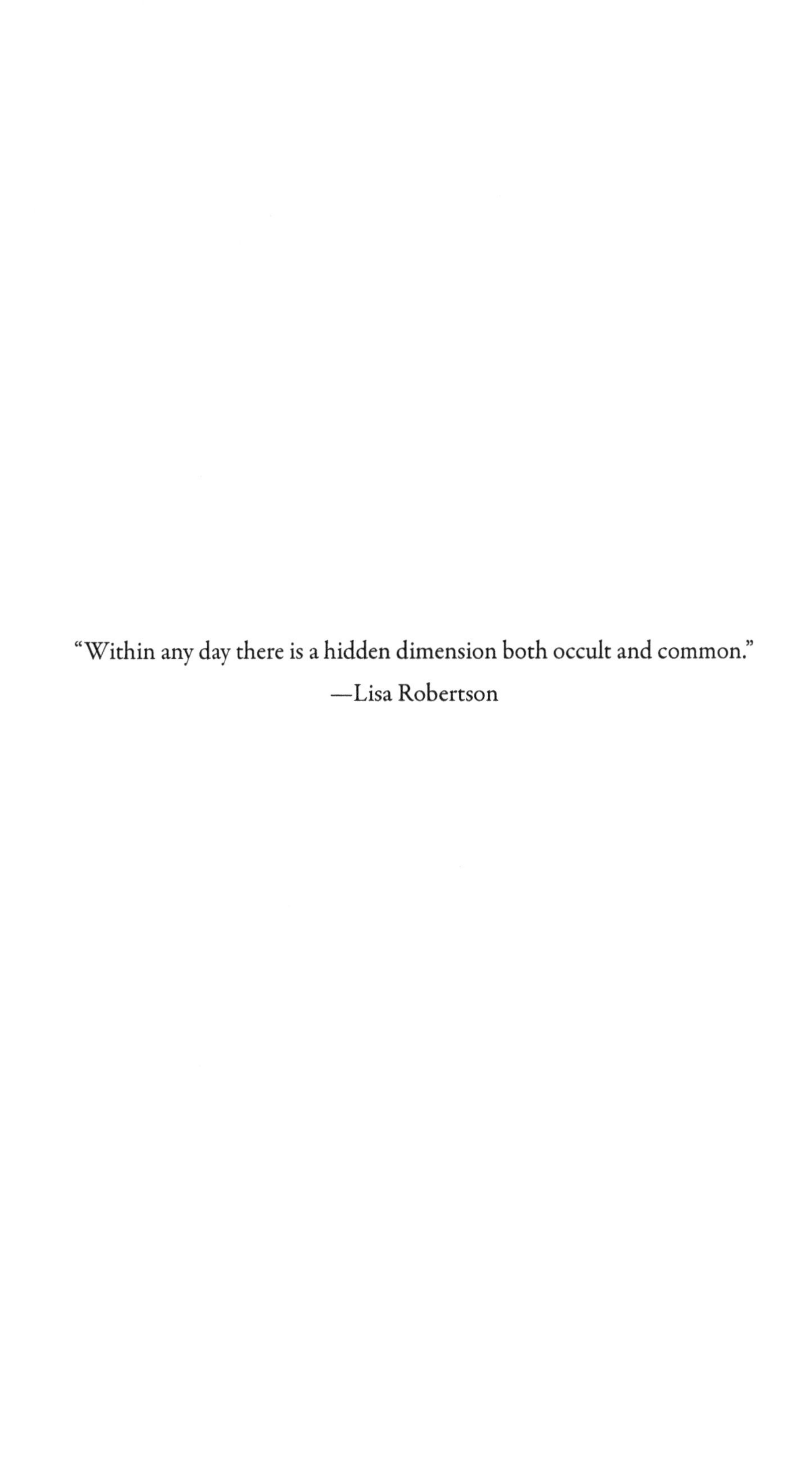

"Within any day there is a hidden dimension both occult and common."
—Lisa Robertson

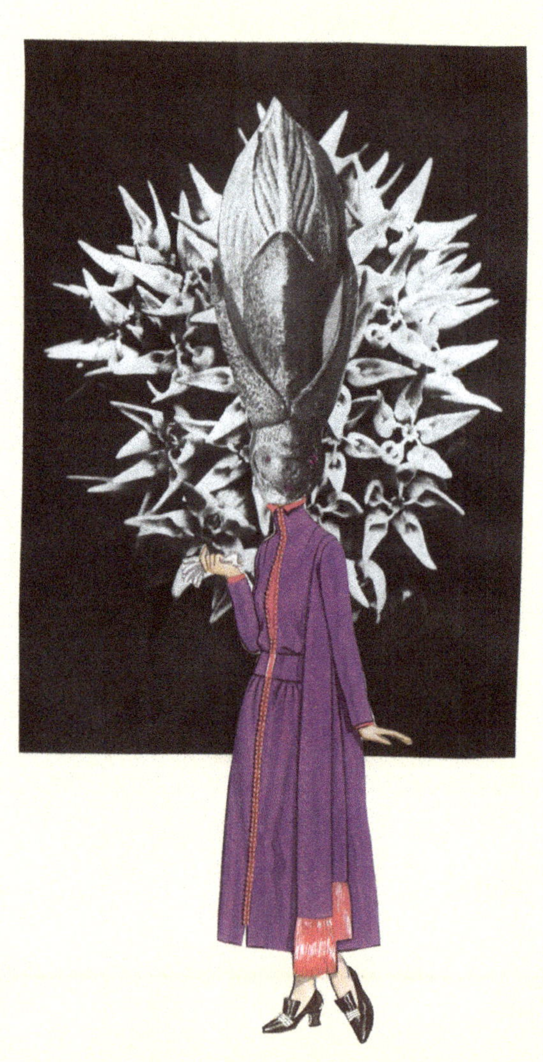

Becoming Swarm

"I feel as if I have an aspen groove that stretches from my stomach to my throat. Sometimes I can hardly speak for trying to hush those leaves."
—*The Witch of Eye*, Kathyrn Nuernberger

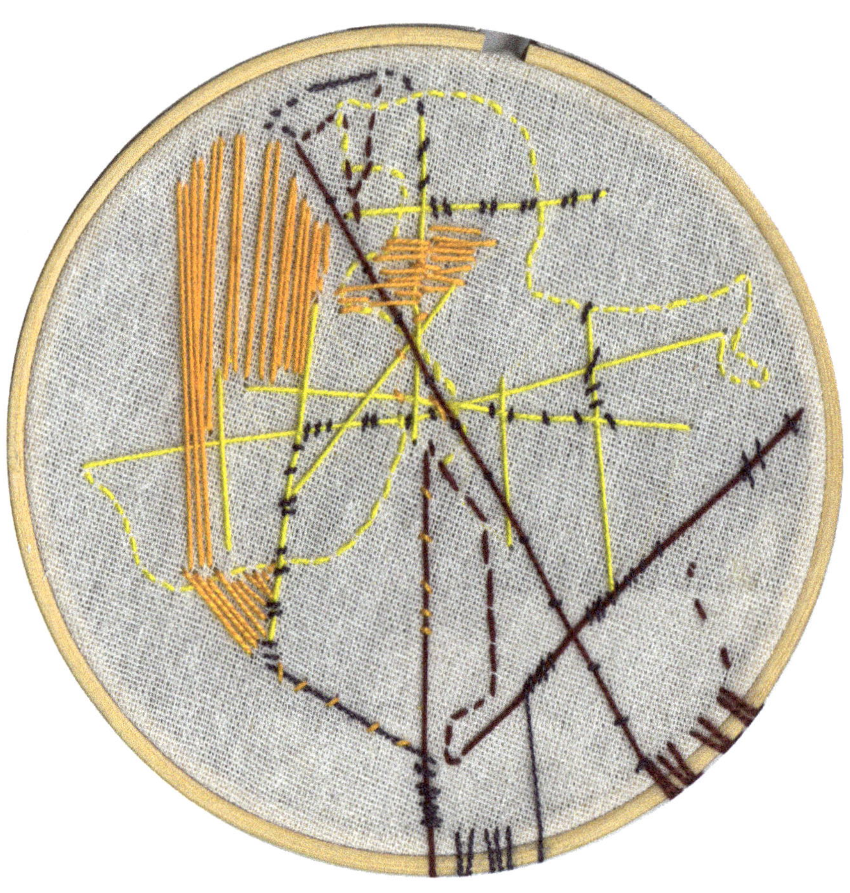

Planchette

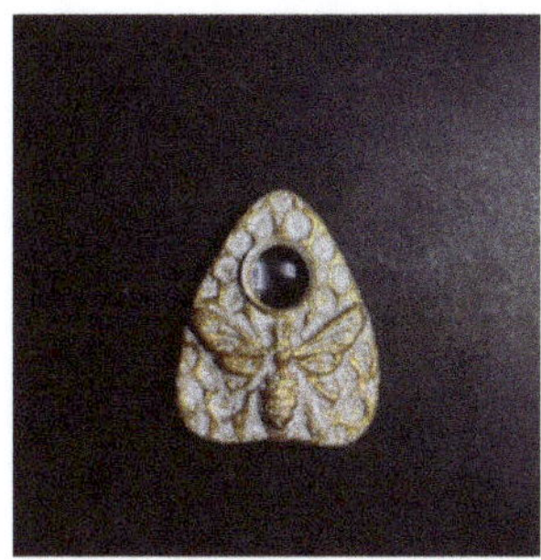

I sought to enter the hive.

To engage with séance as a form of research. An act of calling forth, a way of uncovering the feminine. Not to speak *as*, but to speak alongside. Not to decode or decipher but to create a cacophony. A woven tongue of One.

The collaged poetess as source text. The she as sorceress.

She as the earth in the mouth spilling forth being. She the rooted and ever rooting bloom of lineage. As the soil and the soiled.

Speaking from her mouth of a bee.

She speaks as hive, as poet/goddess, as source of origin, and of our organs.

She is Agnes Martin. She is Yvie Oddly. She is Ana Mendieta. She is Hannah Hoch. She is Lorna Simpson. She is Etel Adnan. She is Jinkx Monsoon. She is Chi Chi DeVayne.

I carry her palimpsest voice in my voice. From the deep cathedral of my mouth, she brings forth light. She speaks. She shines upon my page.

I sought to enter her uprising.

You enter a temple space when you enter a poem.

You enter a hive.

The archive of my insect body is swarming open my mouth to a tunnel in the narrative the bees are channeling.

I sought to enter her archive.

To lean up against embankment of self.

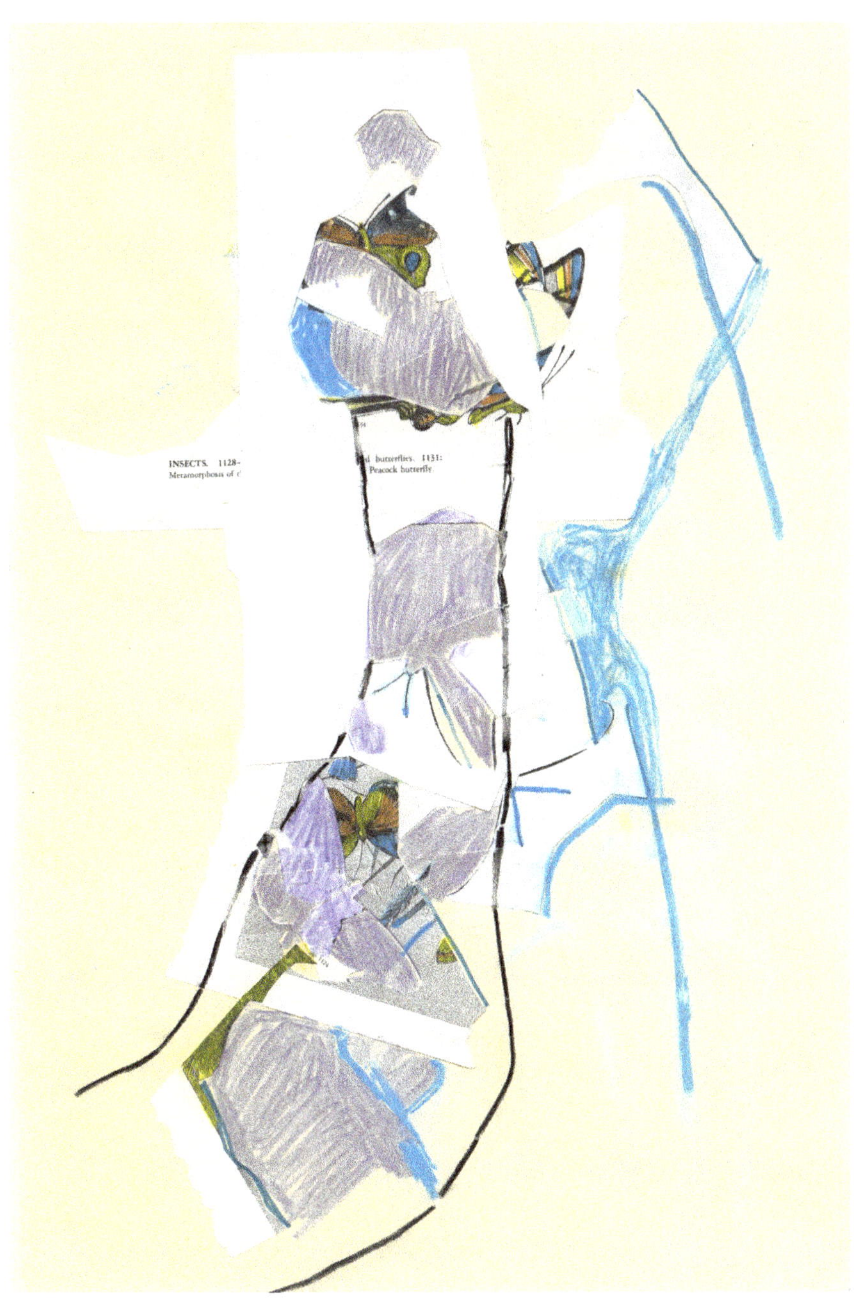

INSECTS. 1128-
Metamorphosis of c
butterflies. 1131:
Peacock butterfly.

She Who Hems from Source: An Introduction

A text is woven ritual. A textile of thought.

I stood for an hour meditating, attuning to the subtleties of my body, and at the end of that hour noticed a slight movement. I spent the next hour exaggerating this movement throughout the performance space. My gesture was a rubbing between thumb and forefinger. I exaggerated this movement of plucking an invisible thread from the ground and extending it into the air. In my writing I found the disparate cultivation of the bird. Found influences (twigs, threads, moss) into the curation of the nest (form, ascension, boundedness). I extended this metaphor into writing: the way in which textual threads (sentences, insights) develop across the page. I thought about gravity and ascension in a piece of writing and drew the following mark: ^^^^^^^^. The hem.

When I researched the etymology of the word "hem," I discovered the word "home" embedded beneath it, in its root system. And the word "selvedge," first named a "self-edge." From there I saw the thread (as a form of linguistic migration, or as a form of sentencing), and the nest (language as a dwelling place, or a refuge for disparate migratory elements). Performance, stitch, led me on a path of poetic discovery—from a movement my body signaled—a hem, directing my mind toward what it could not speak.

Performance lets me view my own body/page. It lets the body speak, in its own nonverbal, non-narrative, un-translated language. A conversation happens. The throat is reformed. The body announces. The vocal cords pronounce. The habitat of the poem becomes the relationship between the page and the body. The habitat of the poem, a refuge.

The tongue, small snake, is rooted in the mouth (a cathedral). It is both imprisoned and free. The teeth bite and bare the tongue, hemming the tongue to its home. A snake has a forked tongue. To make speech multiplicitous (literal & metaphorical at once). This fork makes transformation possible. It brings its speaker to a crossroads where two realms touch (inside & outside, silent & spoken, latent & manifest). Each speech act is an act of divination, emerging from the cathedral, placing floral/lingua at the altar. Swallowing back. Cecilia Vicuna's "spit temple" is this mouth.

To repeat is to open oneself to a form of prayer, your words, thoughts, actions, create patterns, develop grooves, call out to what is invisible. To see what we have been petitioning.

I hung four white bed sheets around the four sides of a cherry picker (that wooden scaffolding that is used to hang lights from the ceiling). You could see inside the space built by the four sheets where I balanced on my stomach on the ladder of the cherry picker stitching "text" (migration patterns of narrative is what I called it) through the front and back of the white cloth. This performance lasted for an hour and while the external view (a line of black or red thread moving through to the front of the sheet) looked extremely minimal, the acrobatics on the inside of the sheets—I spent the entire hour in the air, hooking my arms and legs in various configurations onto the ladder of the cherry picker—was physically excruciating.

When I come to the page, to narrative (I define narrative as the trajectory or propulsion of a piece of text), I think in terms of a front-stitch and a back-stitch, or as having an undercurrent of movement (an unseen or unsaid intensity—what happened between the sheets). As a reader, I consider both the front stitch—what is said in a text—the conscious parts, and the back stitch—the secret narrative trajectory—the current that is unknown or known only subconsciously to the writer during composition.

In the summer of 2003 I gathered old maps, sewing patterns, sea charts, knitting needles, a spinning globe, and a long black ribbon with the word *air* stitched onto it. I was interested in the relationship between the knitting needle and the compass, the parallel of sea charts and sewing patterns, the gendered orientation of travel and exploration, the "magic trick" of breathing onto the ribbon, flipping it over for the audience and finding it labeled "air." The breath as *air*. I stitched four white bed sheets together and covered them in sea charts and sewing patterns.

I came to recognize the hem as a display of mapping: how a bird maps its migration (the needle poking through the sheet as its beak), how navigators map a landscape (physical cartography), how the fabric patterns themselves map an outfit (or continental drift), and how words map a sentence (the thread generally moving from left to right). I thought of a poem as a demonstration of call and response, of region and localization, of echo and refrain. And the architecture of the hem as continents, dresses, sea charts, and navigations, in recollection.

Repetition is an act of duration. We repeat a specific gesture for long periods of time, one hour, two hours, to see what new sparks arise from our sacred petitioning. As sound or action progresses, the thump or drone of the repetition begins to bind us to a new experience of space and time. Individual boundaries dissolve as performers/readers/speakers merge into one acting animal, bound by our collective rhythms.

To stitch: to pull something together in context, to combine two unlike things in association. A stitch as metaphor, the near and far touching, tentatively. A temporary outpouring of relationship. As long as the stitch will hold.

Channel

Thus spoke   the violet
and spoke the   trebling
in a pyre of shapes   spoke
a wild bull   and slain
the fire breathing woman   self propagating
like a water lily or locust   her sun

And spoke the ravine   inside her seed
bespoke the river   ravished with blood
inside her graveyard   and her
underbrush already   revelatory
pomegranates sewn   to her cloth

Spoke to the sea   and to
the rabbits   to the wild-eyed
forest nymph uncovered   by the telling
spoke the aftermath   and her successors
leaves and berries   sprung

And thus there were no more   red hangings
and no more trees lined   with blood
the holly and the kerm-oak   and the muttering
soil   courted a new curse

And it was then that   the ground
broke open   to swallow them
it did not come from the sky

But spoke deep inside   her insurrection
        an ovum
      in a field of   lupines
manifested by snows   of early spring

    And bespoke the ever opening   tulip
          eaten by women   as passage
reborn as ghosts   reborn as flower husks
        as emblems as palpable and holy
      unholy   with mulberry dripping
                from their throats

    And something in the language   pulsing
standing three stones deep   in her under story
in her carrying forth   of bodily imprint

        Thus spoke plants and flowers
      to her on every hill   and hive

        Thus spoke   the channel

          Ensnaring the physical

            Mineral thing
          Seeding   genetic patterns
            blaze   and veins

    Where language spoke   red toned,
    Spoke a brush fire all organs bridged

Spoke a flower inside her flower's telling   spoke
          corpse   of grief   spoke infinite
                    Strums in the heatspace

          Spoke caesura,
     remote and mountainous   inside her body
               a petalite more specious
               awake   (below below)

As Long as the Stitch will Hold

I think of writing as part séance.

I think of writing as part architectural nest building.

I have gathered the threads. I have gathered the circumstance. Now I am knee-deep in the reeds. Now I am covered in milkweed fluff. Now I am a witch drowning. Now I am a Goddess rising.

Now I am a witch casting a spell.

I made my descent into the underworld, into the understitch, under the tongue, grief stricken, silent. I made my descent beneath the veil. I sought my sister there.

*

When my sister passed away in 2017, I went back to my hometown to her mother's house to help sort out details for her funeral. Her mother monitored my every move, asking if I needed water, tea, coffee. Asking if I was too warm, too cold, too tired, too awake. Asking if I wanted the window open, a blanket. Wondering if I was pregnant (no, just in my 40s with thyroid disease). Wondering if I was experiencing early menopause. Telling me how I would regret not having a baby, how I would be haunted by my loneliness in old age.

I sought the wisdom of women, the alchemical chamber of the body. I went inside the cavern of the mouth, cavern of the earth, cavern of the womb, cavern of the hive, the dark space where creation becomes. I became a Lady of the animals, a pythoness, a bee. The threads knotted in my throat. Each dream I had was an embroidery.

I stitched to talk to thunderstorms inside my sister.

I stitched to gather an aesthetic. Kate Bush in her red, billowy-sleeved dress. Marshes. Floods. Marie Redonnet's *Hotel Splendid*. Marilyn Robinson's *Housekeeping*. Train tracks. Train cars. The dream of hopping on and racing toward a new horizon, a certain kind of loneliness. Existential loneliness. And independence. The exhaustion and resourcefulness of deep silence. The train tracks just across the street from my childhood house. The trees there too.

After her death, I found a small safe broken open inside my sister's bedroom. The paramedics searched for heroin there. But the core of her was not drugs. The core of her was an image of kittens. A purple pouch full of gemstones. My sister was a lock of hair. She was Hungarian tarot cards. She was a picture of her parents on their wedding day. She was a burlesque matchbox. She was a collection of stamps.

I found a flight pattern, a ritual, a trace, a beehive, an infinite knot, a way to write and revise, and revise again. A way to resentence the sentence my sister and I had been handed. To change the story by telling our story. To enter a wound. To face it again and again until we are transformed by it. Until we see it clearly and move it through our body.

My sister and I are not related. Not by blood. But we are the same age, and we are both named Andrea. Her mother and my father married when we were 10. I always thought of her as part doppelganger, part mirror-image. I was jealous that her mother fled with her in the night, brought her to America. For me it was the opposite. My mother fled to California but left me behind in Chicago with my dad. My sister's mother is dramatic, emotional, talkative, whereas my own mother is pragmatic, quiet, and emotionally reserved.

I began stitching lines instead of writing them.

A line is a descent, an expedition into the underworld, into the root system of language. It marks an act of sensing, of perception translated by the realm of the mouth.

I titled the stitches, *Séance of the Bees*.

I think of bees as the narrative force of the stitching. The voice or sound or energy that marks the flight pattern of my asemic lines.

I modeled the lines on bee flight patterns. Figure 8s and other erratic movements to and from the hive. I traced a field of flowers inside the roof of my mouth as sentence. Felt its bloom. The drops of dew. Blood and other eroticisms of fluid. The nectar of the line.

My sister died three days after her 38th birthday. She overdosed three times and was saved, before the fourth and final overdose, which took place in the middle of the night in front of her bathroom mirror. She was covered in water.

I think of Emily Dickinson's *certain slant of light*. How it falls across the page, or cloth, as insight.

This is an act of séance. How an essay calls embers to surface.

I began to think about viruses in narrative. How various hatreds or phobias arise from and spread through the spell cast by a single sentence or story repeating and replicating itself throughout a culture, how origin stories, mythologies, and fairy tales unfold to reinforce cultural ideologies.

I thought of my sister. An immigrant. Without access to adequate mental health care. At the receiving end of her mother's co-dependency. A woman alone and in pain.

The channel we traveled to meet each other. Our bee flight path. International, over an ocean, across electricity, a storm. Against an abyss of language. Our bodies tightly woven in shared clothing and bedrooms. Our tongues unacquainted with one another's syllabic sounds.

A divide. That which severs. That which disrupts. Passage as a rupture or reworking of a wound. A mark, as in a scar. A suture. To see the passage as intermediary zone.

In Engadin mythology the human soul is said to turn into a bee upon death. I began to create embroideries as a way to speak. To grieve for my sister and to grieve for the bees, becoming silent, becoming swarm.

Thread pierces the front of a piece of cloth, severs the mark between what is seen and unseen, as it resurfaces, gathers a bit of what is invisible. This backstitch is how a line loops the ineffable into what it speaks. A gap, hesitation, caesura, wound, lacuna, tear, marked by this piercing.

Andrea, with whom I was thrown together under such bizarre circumstances, knows my heart's home. Just as I will always know, and recognize, the heart of her.

A row, a doctrine, a division, a limit, a gesture, a mark, a horizon, a lineage, a tongue. Multiple lines becoming maps, nests, homes, patterns, rituals, boundaries, containers, passages, rooms.

The palm of the hand is a map of lines. Two sisters speak not in tongues, but in double helixes. Patterns of movement. Passages from foreign language textbooks. Tethered. Doubled to a mirror image, an Andrea, our DNA.

All language, but perhaps especially poetic language, contains a front stitch and a back stitch. The wound and its utterance.

Light enters the wound. The door of one sentence closes and the door of another sentence opens. The period as a point of puncture.

An entry between one realm to the next.

The mouth acts as nest to bind together the threads of being. The self (or I) as needle which pricks the air with sound. *I,* a bird's beak, a boundary. The mouth, continent of self, and all that remains outside of the self, as other, as air. What is swallowed versus what is sung out.

My sister, a woman from Budapest, Hungary, intercepted my flight pattern. Sang out inside my mouth. Sang out as a twined self. As my name. As another being that was my being.

A sentence, an embroidery, a lineage, a rhizome, a thread, a divining rod, a root, a branch, a wingspan, a twig, a nest, a woven structure, a pattern, a repetition, a ritual, a metaphor, a eulogy, a song.

I resurface. I return from the underworld. By way of this line.

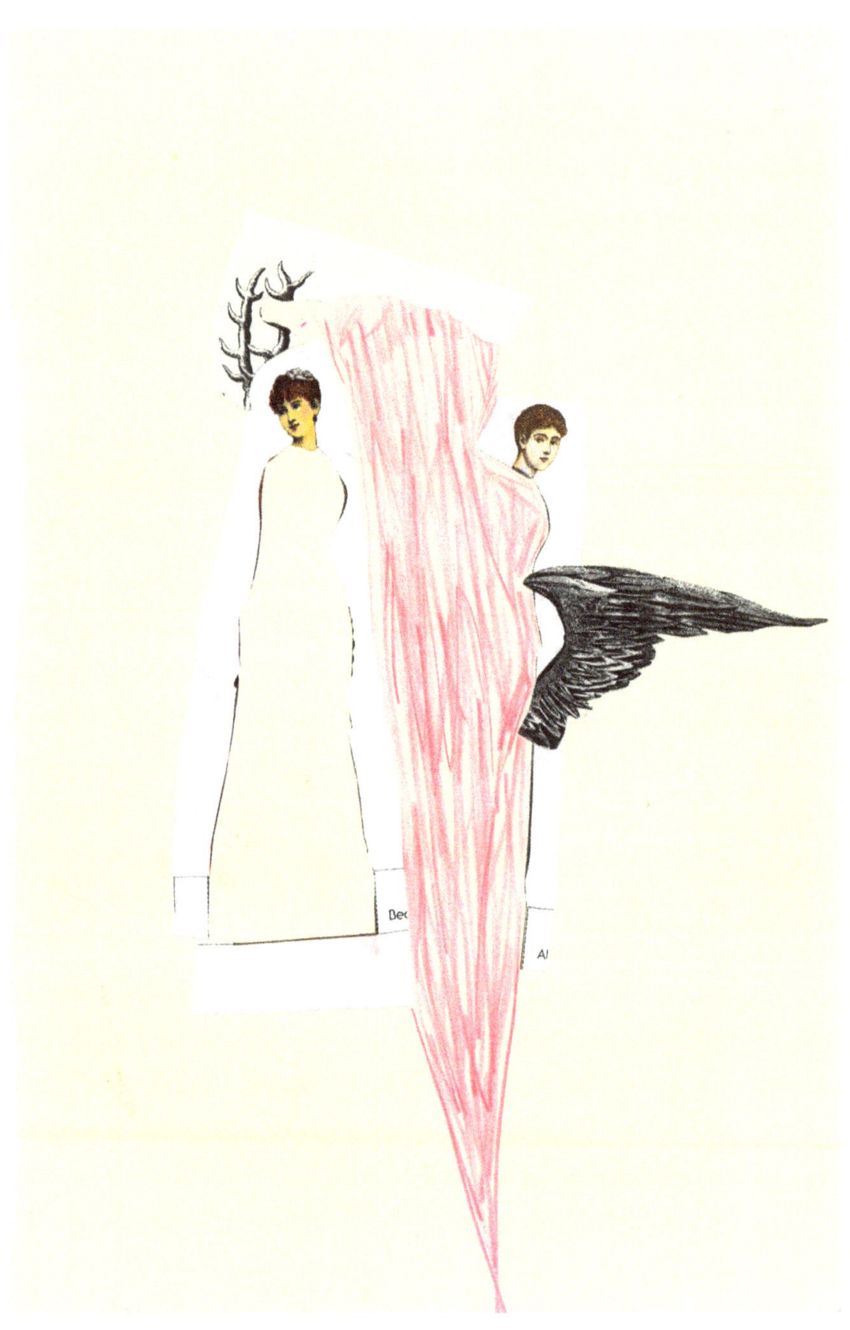
Bea
Al

Structure of a Flower

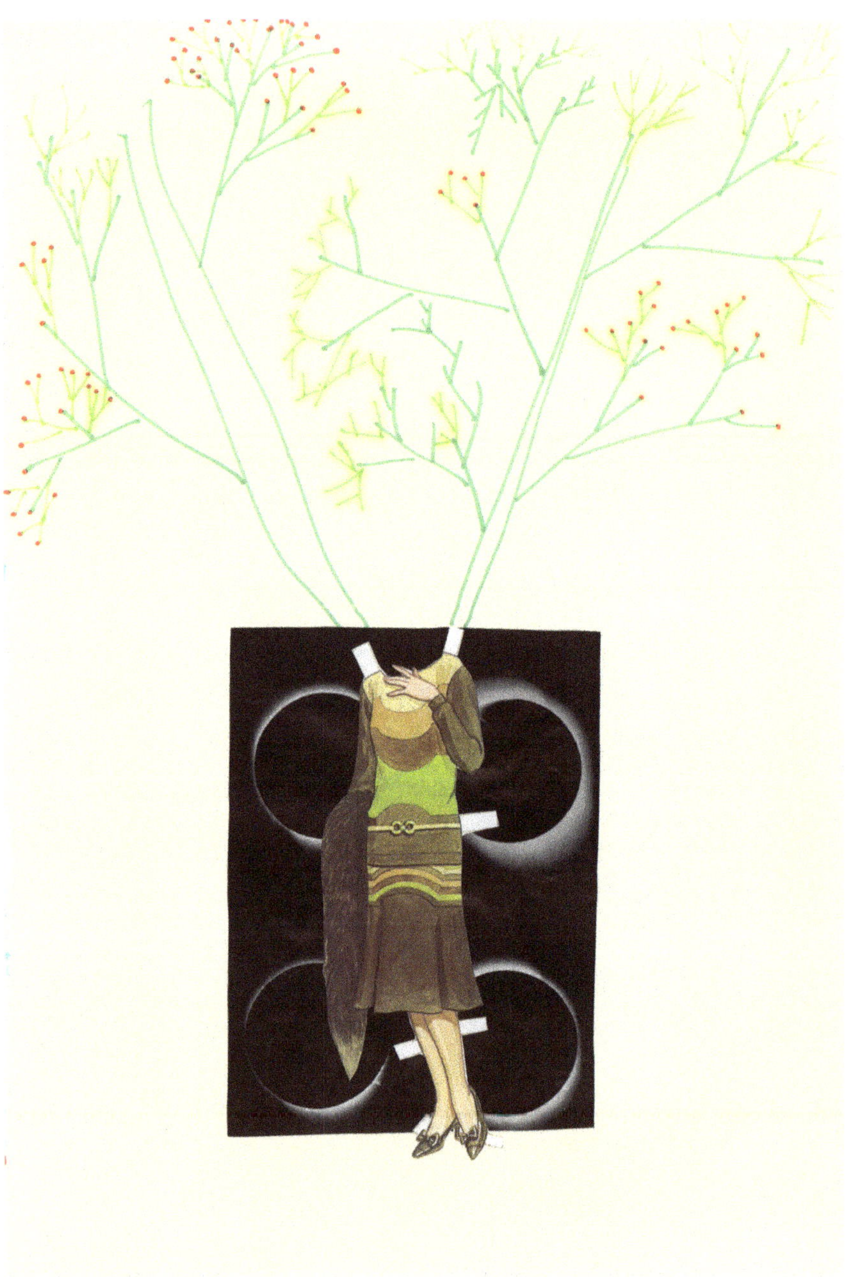

The Way the Language Was

The day the deer died,
I was alive in my house.
I was alive in a watery field
of glaciers. In the realm
of birchwood in my throat.
The day the robins wept, the day
foxes ran from the woods on fire.
I was alive in a decade. Sometimes
dreaming of another region
was my religion. It was
a place before trees, prior
to the flame. When the deer died,
I was in my house dreaming. Then
the drought came. Cessation
of sound. Flames as red as apples
lodged inside my throat hissing.

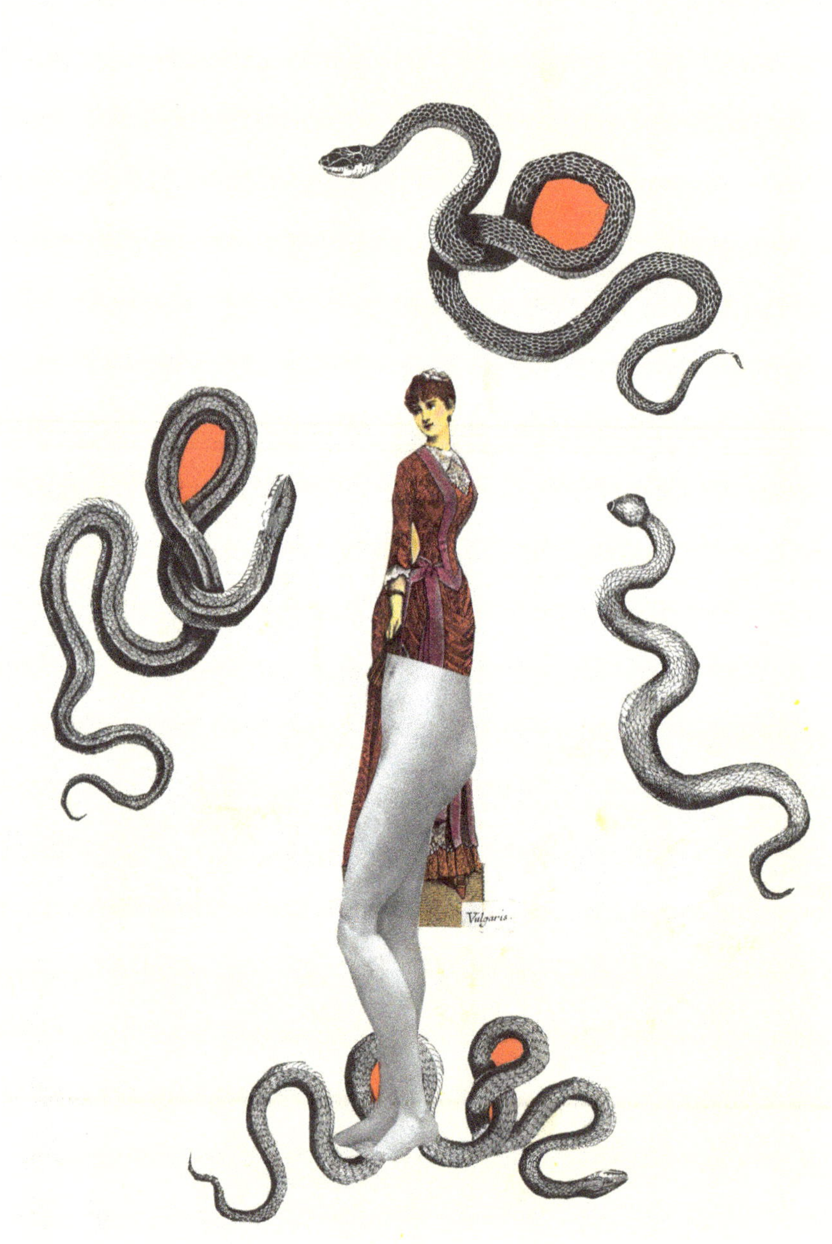
Vulgaris

The Structure of a Flower: Stigma

Not a mirror
Air / water / fish / bird,
Ruin of the human body.
A site of rain.
Think genomes
doubled-over.
An abandoned
house grown
over with plants. Lists.
Alphabets.
Folded out. Transcribing.
Shadows of birds fly over.
9:35 A.M.

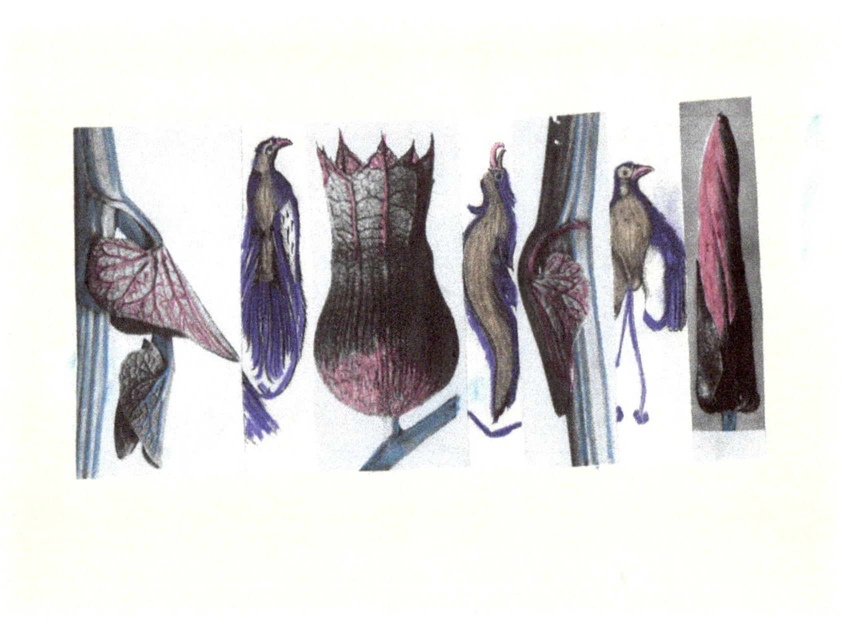

The Way the Language Was

The way the heat was
The way the migrating butterfly was
The way the sky was
The way the bee was
The way the garden was
The way the rape was
The way the hive was
The way the hand taking the body's temperature was
The way the cactus was
The way the symphony was
The way the water-strider was
The way the sympathy was
The way the country was
The way the house was
The way the soil was

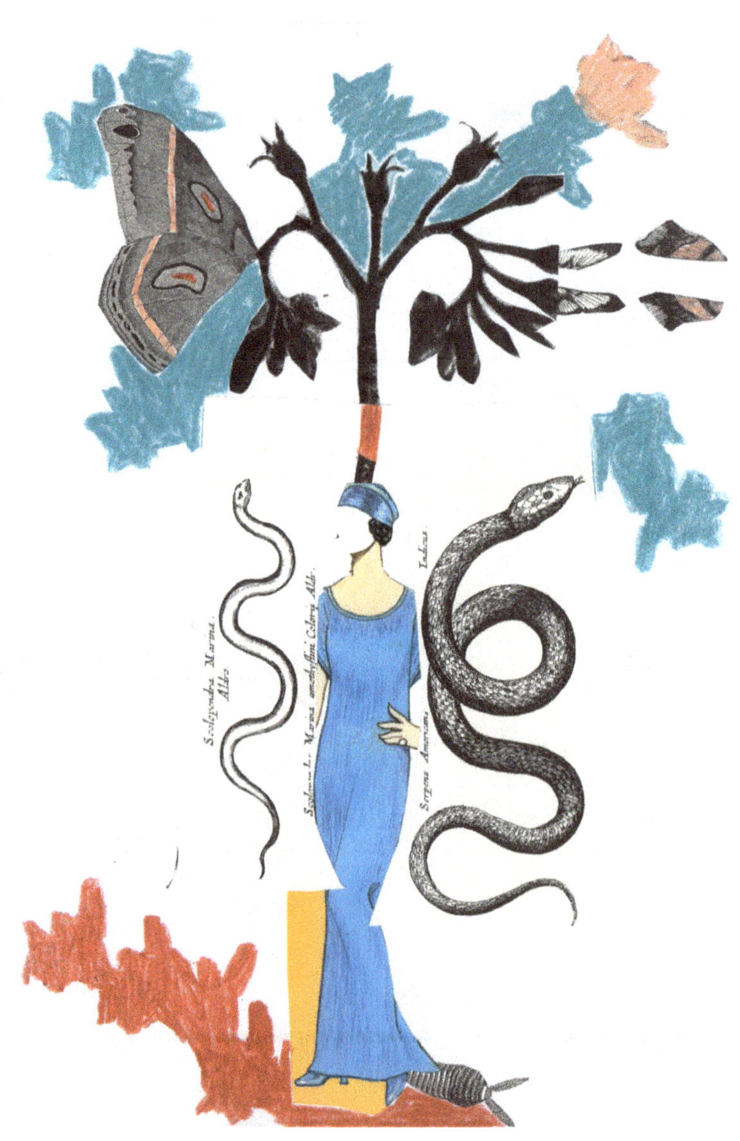

Scolopendra Marina. Alba
Scolopendra Marina amethystini Coloris. Alb.
Indicus.
Serpens Americanus.

The Structure of a Flower: Sepal

Pastoral etymology,
Terrain of human and nonhuman elements
Sun. The trees. I in the poem.
Hinges. At the core a loam.
Resonances between brooks, between
branches inside a letter.
An archeological dig to uncover origins
of the Leaf-like. Self-like mouth.
Folds of the tongue a root branching toward sky.
Another doubling organism. Seed pods,
as genitals. When it was mud. When it was
the trees I have seen.

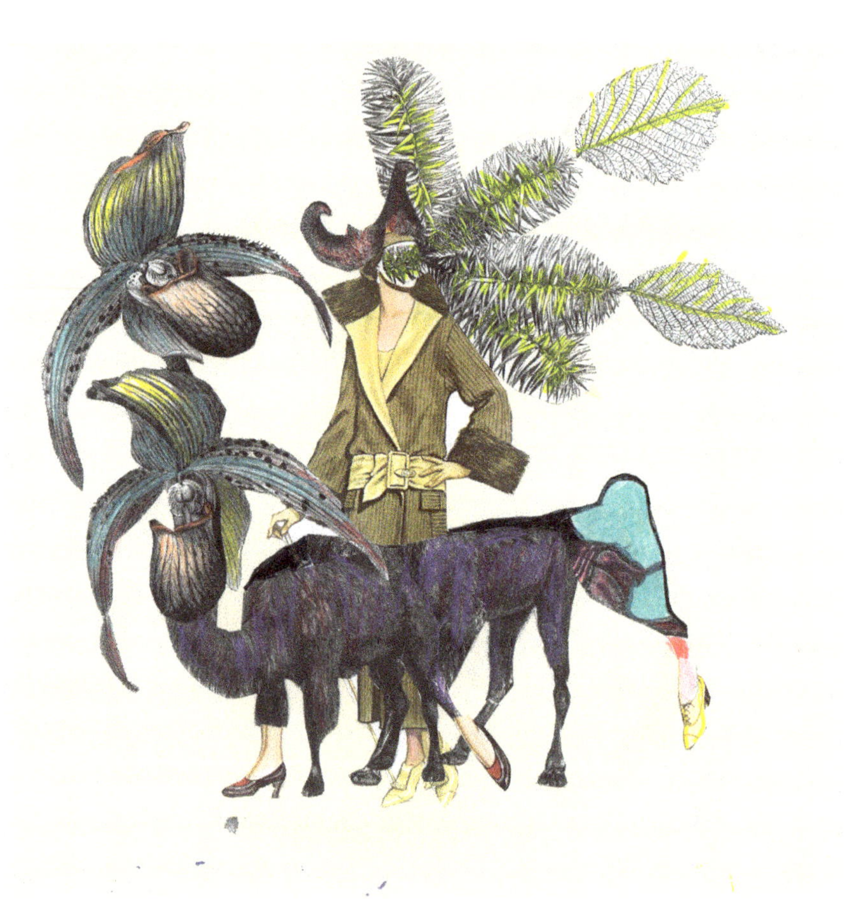

Afterword

A very light lemon self; a self of replication;
a self of galactic hills of the subterranean
womb; a creamy amber yellow self with a
lime throat constricted; a semblance of ash
in the month-of-the-ash-self; the growth of
grass, the first witches of the year, the first
bees; a creamy yellow self swallowing pond
stones to tenderly sprout a stock of the new
self; a golden flower self; a fire revelation
self of being the birth-tree, the silver fir, the
unborn sea; the unborn; a creamy white
self with light green throat asking clouds to
mother, then weather; a velvety black wine
red self licking mulch; an ivy-twined, fir cone
scarred self, the myth of which in return;
in reference to the first day of the year, the
first reference dedicated to the cult of the
flower corpse returned in a boat, floated
down the Rhone to Alyscamps at Arles; an
over-examined self, a pale amethyst violent
self with a pale yellow throat of wasps; a self
of bees and eighteenth century antiquary; a
written self, the "lofty one" transcribed as a
self wound, a woven self with a green throat
with stones in the swollen thorax, stones in
the split spine; stones in the lingering of the
gut; a pink or poppy red self and a yellow

green throat channeling pre-Columbian bees; a lavender pink self in the early morning ash-groves, in the early morning pandemonium, fading until the lavender remains on all edges; green throat becoming greener internal wilderness. A subdued self, pricked into cactus seeds. A luminous pink decaying self; a pale self burning away; is the third tree; is the third tree composted; is the third tree in the moss. A creamy lemon self emergent as a yellow green throat of trees. Very pale lemon self with yellow forested throat; elegiac self; dark red self with sorrowful green throat, plucks berries from the mouths of birds; it is late for the nameless self; onn; ura; a self lighted on the hills in return; a coronation; a coronation violet self with green throat; formed into ferns; no reference to her own forest; an attractive melon pink self threaded, overturned log self of sounding forth; a bee-loud glade selfishness. A deeply seamed red and medium yellow bicolor or polychrome selfless self, the orange self; a rose pink self with white midribs; self of acumen; self of carrying forth; a clear golden yellow scared self, free blooming self; a bright light yellow self; resonating sanctity; a coral amber peach self with a yellow green throat listless and listening to a pink self with a green throat slit; a free blooming self; a self of the ingrained field of sleeting; a newly sprouted self, deep

yellow self with cream midrib and terrestrial
longing for uprooted golden flowers; a
purplish red self at the close of the mouth;
a tiny melon pink self with a green throat
which has become fir-tipped; a self under the
tongue; a self the blend of dusty rose forked
tongues; an orange yellow self with a golden
throat; an orange yellow self with an orange
throat full of deep water; a dark black red
self buzzing with a green throat harvesting
mulch hunted by elk; gathering stones to
heave into herself; a clear blue lavender blue
self with a lime throat; a light orange self in
the semblance of abysmal fields at night; a
scarlet red self with a yellow throat which
supplies a carrot orange self an olive green
throat; an avowed self; a self as new sentience

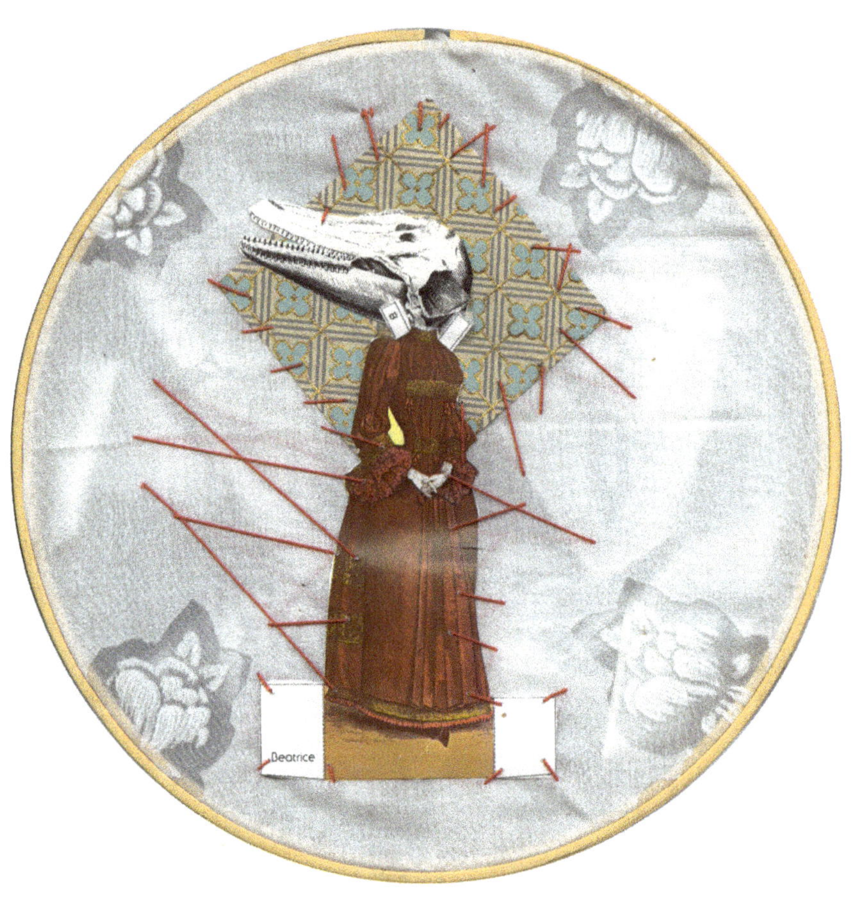

Beatrice

Hive Song

Swarm / An Arm

Agape

To let a

channel   charnel ground an ontological revision

bloom upon opening bloom
opening renditions of form

yellow lip of daffodil in the high mountain desert of breath
sound makes a storm unfolding

on this occasion we worry

over air

what arises in

inhalation of other

selves and cells

how contaminated

distant bringing

we did not see our need

for boundary delimits

our interior

examined

petition

to be bought

    and sold

        to be made barren by want

            be made unholy

by the diabolical book

    of our own invention

        there is no end

            until flame comes

    all the leaves

        and feathers of birds

            the fur of animals, their paws

        and eyes

fallen into ash

    wild herbs, the underworld

            shadows, also gone

of all that is water all that is surrender all that is flower all that is birth all that is
symbiotic all that is embryonic all that is egg all that is oval all that is plant all
that is circular all that is planet

    I keep in my inner orbit

        keep in my seed sphere

          lodged in the gut of me

lodged in the throat

we choose with

mouths, expirations

scent glands

queen bees lodged

in fallopian tubes

insects huddled, draped

in unrest

spores multiplying toward

new generation

held acts of naming

marking

surfaces ineffable

seed pod nest structure architecture from which

we emerge

to imagine all future openings, the forms of being, resistance
of loom bursting forth. the seepage. warning the clotted blood. warning the
wound which stops the flow altogether

to return. to return to this state of passage. from the underworld into light.
from the before into the after of light. and to hold each within us

                                        as firmament

            on this occasion we eat grass
                                                to survive an onslaught
                    language a crossroads as blessing

                                        as a cathedral inside our mouth
                        marsh of saliva carving out
                                tunnel cavern curvature undergrowth

                        wilderness lives inside this mouth
                                        descent

                    into dark asemic woods of writing

            agape
                                                to let the hand

    a swarm of murmuration swarm of resonance, of augmentation
    swarm of radiance

                                swarmed to the tender pricked plant
                                swarm to an ending, transfigured
                        agape to

                        gale of resounding vibration of hush in the hum space
                            gale of longing of honey-scented desire in the breeze

                                    peonies, hydrangeas, the color of tulip

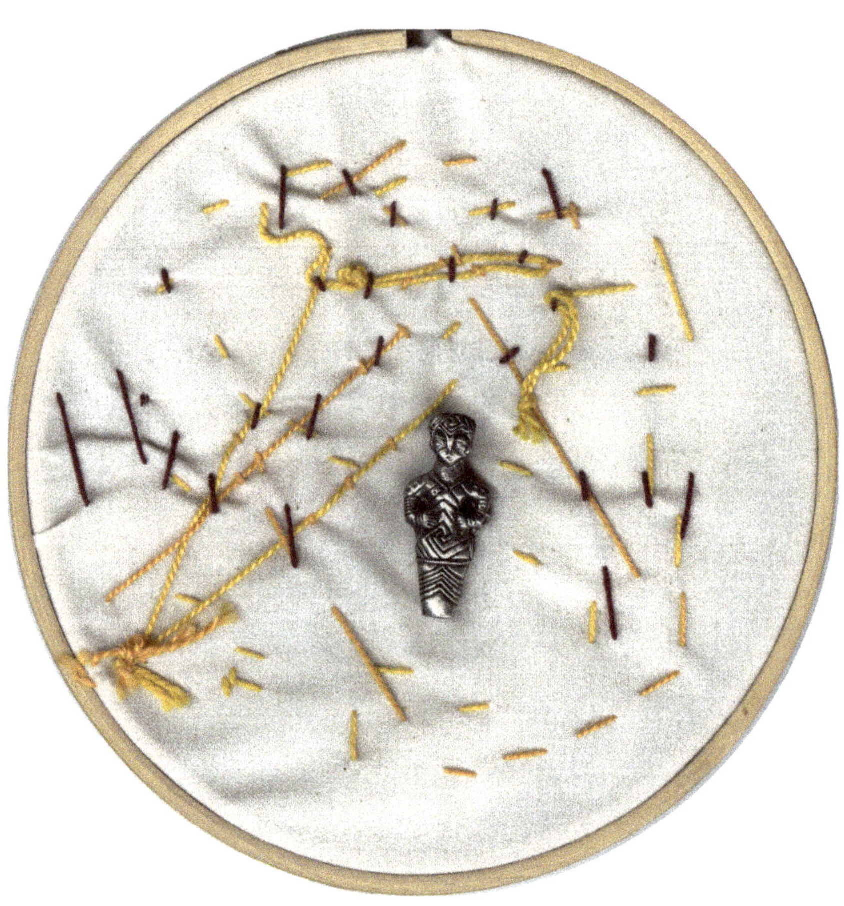

Catacombs

They built a flower from the mutterings of ghosts and enormous quantities of
water, prophetesses of the queer fruit-trees who assumed forms of lightning in
the glorious dark, who drank blood from a cask inside an old oak tree; bespoke
through familiars in the hand of the burning bush

Her blooming femmes
her blooming
                                    articulation

as a pistol
her bees

Vision: I am in a cavernous space with many other people. Being counted off,
non-linearly, eight-hundred ninety-four, fifty-six, seven. We lie on the ground
naked in a shape of a skull, Victorian tableau vivant in the hollows.

In order to perform the ritual one must move as bees move.
Erratic figure 8s and other tremblings at the altar.

A stone is placed at loop's center to form a knot of arrival, from which text arises.

Emerges new weathered sky on the brink of articulation. She exhausts herself.
She emerges. Emerging again, in repetition. Petitioning. She emerges like a
monsoon. Petitioning monthly thread ritual. New moon. Veil-winged. In vales.

Out of the milky whiteness come the grids.

Yellow kaleidoscope of flowers. Unfurled remedy. Creases speak.
                              In the field. In the field.

Dream:

Song of first unfolding   a place a fire something woven   unpetaling
revelation itself   song   of the first tree   song of fur burnt
pollen   not song   but slaying of the buried   of the charred   bespoke
     flora ashen   first to bloom sighing

                                   Her bees hum a governance.

Once I was a corpse beneath the sea. Now I am called to awaken. Now I am
called from discontent, from the dampness to reframe what is not my labor.

Sight: When it is time to return she hums a midwife insect. She hums her
obtaining / carries phenomena from the beginning / first slaying of the seed-
pod she used to / carry I would willingly carry /from my private séance I had
permission / in their possession from my invisible / to do so I had made a note

White space

                                   is

          the

underbelly

of her bees.

Site: In the field. In the field of yellow, golden flowers. Of milkweed. Of aster in bloom.

Sky a further channel. Cloud and constellation texts. The catacomb. Oh. Omen. Become comb painting.

> She will be carried from the flowers of one language to another. She will be carried downstream to a cave at the edge of the river. Feel behind her stone pathway and mossy roof, inner cathedral singing with the voice of a witch.

Women are an omen opened.

Inside the realm of Persephone. Inside the realm.

Your women circle chanting. It is above my pay grade. Above my pay. To gather intel. To pause. *You need your orgasm to be part of your art.*

To practice sewing home in your interior.

Flight Pattern

The first time I saw a flower I was inside my mother's womb. It was yellow daffodils or red tulips. She was tending to grass, so I could be born in deep winter to the blank light of scrying. Tending to the interior of my girl. Part owl. The woman looks inside the soil of her body. The wind a furious wolf outside. The woman tells me. Something about flowers. Something about how they bloom. I rub my hands with chalk. Taste yellow inside my mouth. Wet my unfurling in the light of the water's flow.

A femme is an open channel. A meta pattern through which to see the world. The woman tells me I grew up across the street from a river. A nest of mud. Maybe a single pearl wedged somewhere in the shadows. *I was a plant. An animal. I was air.* I was a cave opening into a mountain. An immensity. I saw a cathedral deep in the hollows of my heart space. I could become a hermit.

The woman tells me breasts and hips and the head an arrow opening toward the sky. Carried in my pockets, in my purse. I place them in my mouth. Or on my abdomen. I plant stones to achieve teleportation. I bury stones in the woods. Place them in the ground, in the river, on the train tracks, in the mud. To place a crease. In the woods across the street from my childhood home. The night sky on top of a cliff. A field of wildflowers. Where I plant my past self. Near the ocean, in California. Without a match to gather roots. Without my entire body. Inside the dream wind pulls my hair like flame. These red-branched veins a series of postcards to various rivers I have known. My femme is

Part soil, part spit. Bordered interior. The part the womb partakes. Etymology of one who awakens the dead. Source tongue; vigilante. One who eats leaves: foliage:

pages of a book: sheets of paper: open plank of forehead. Leaf cutter. Hidden hem. A fem word. From a root translated as the flame of rising ash.

She peers through a glass lens of ice brought down from the mountains.

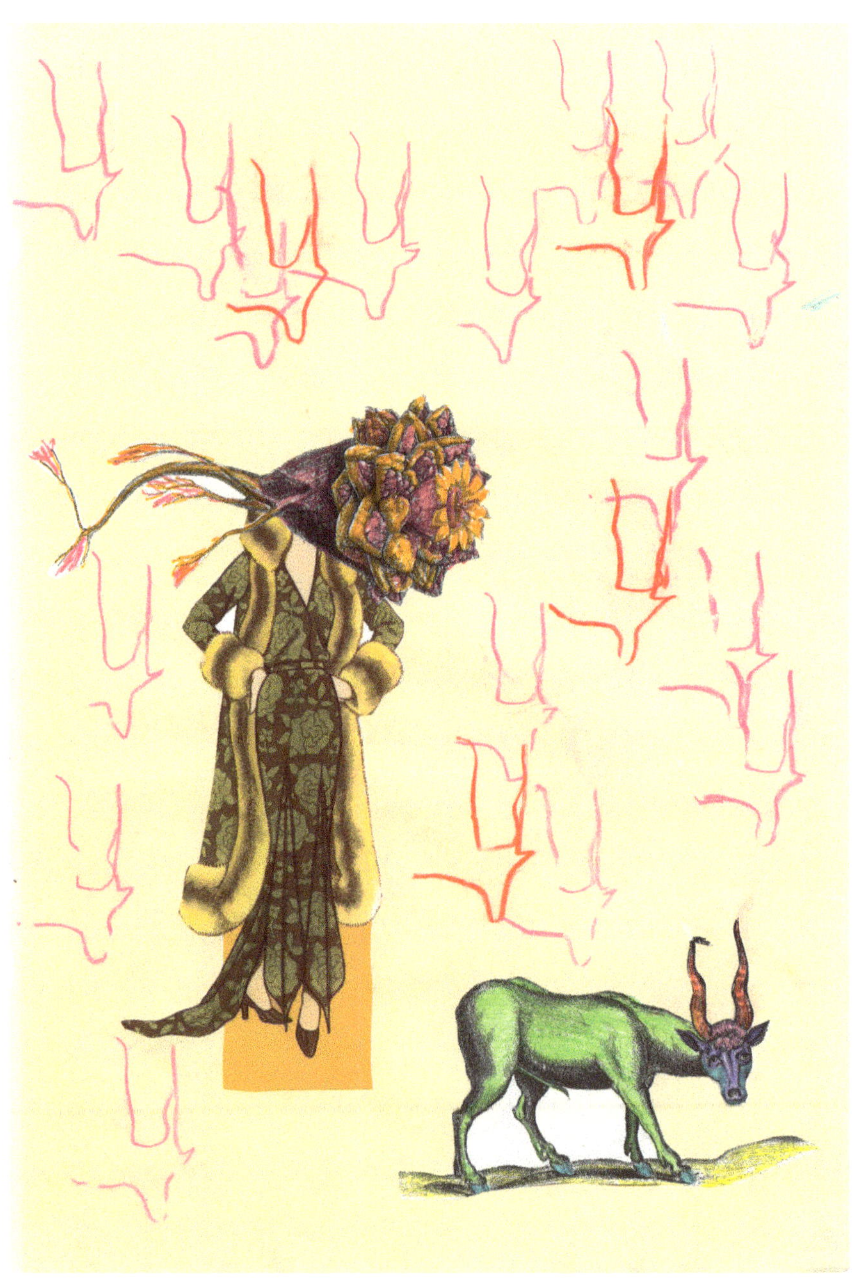

The Bees

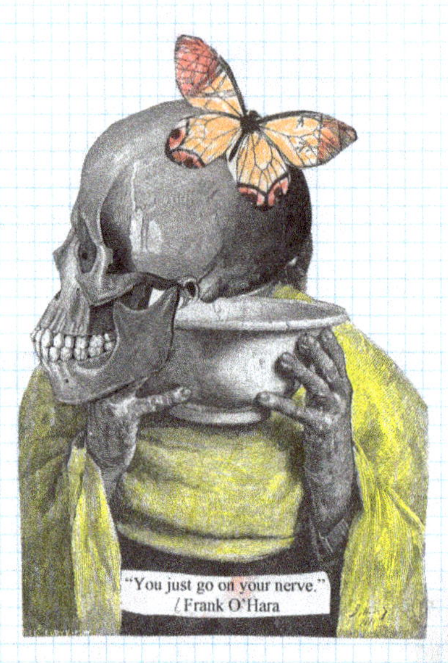

"You just go on your nerve."
/ Frank O'Hara

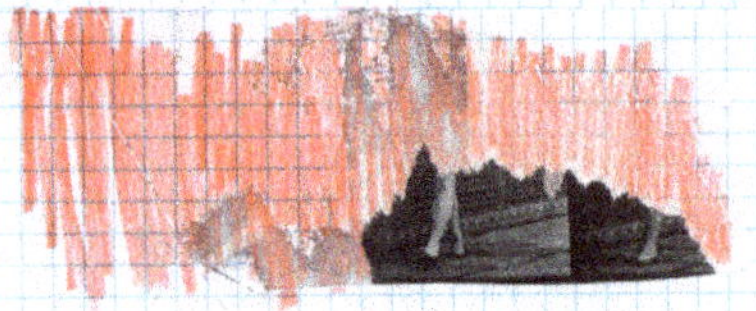

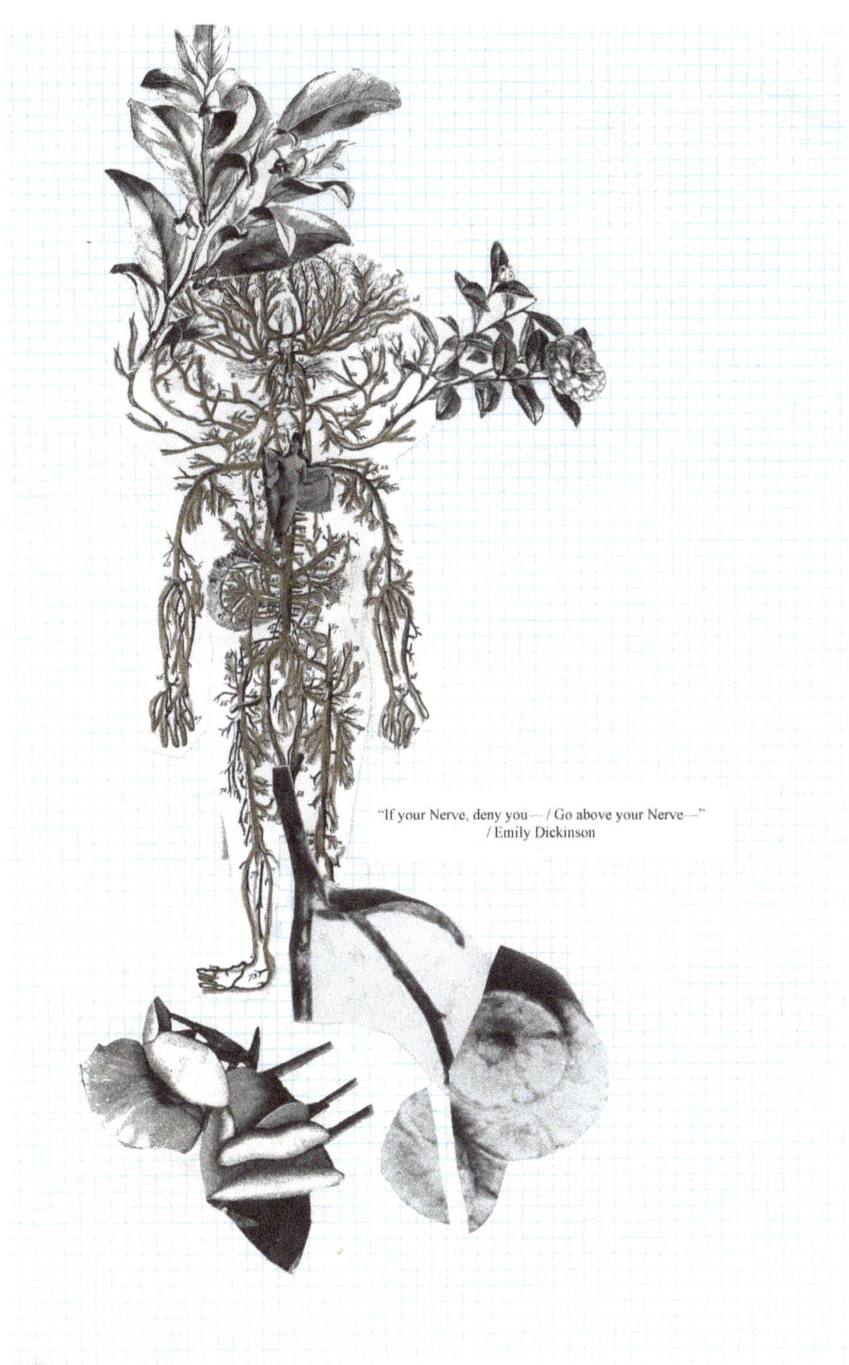

"If your Nerve, deny you— / Go above your Nerve—"
/ Emily Dickinson

"Form was not born from an idea. / It was an idea vanishing."
/ Cecilia Vicuña

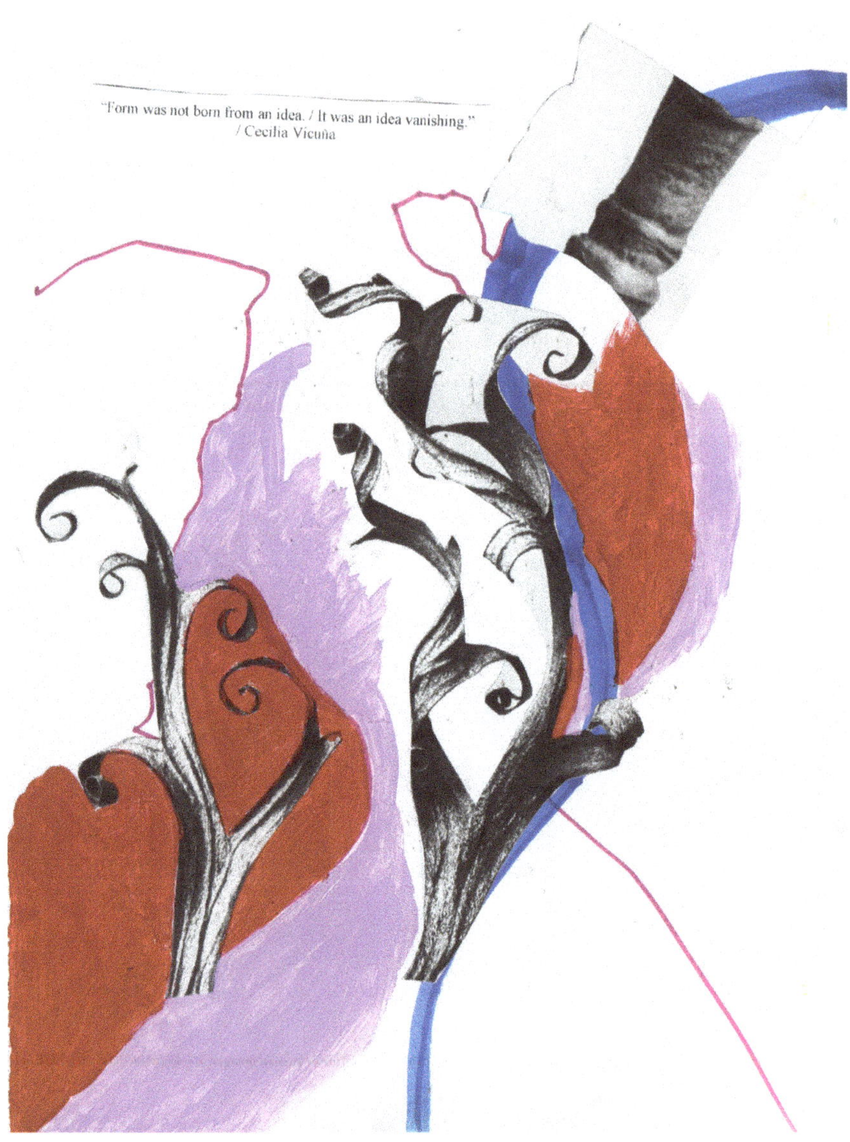

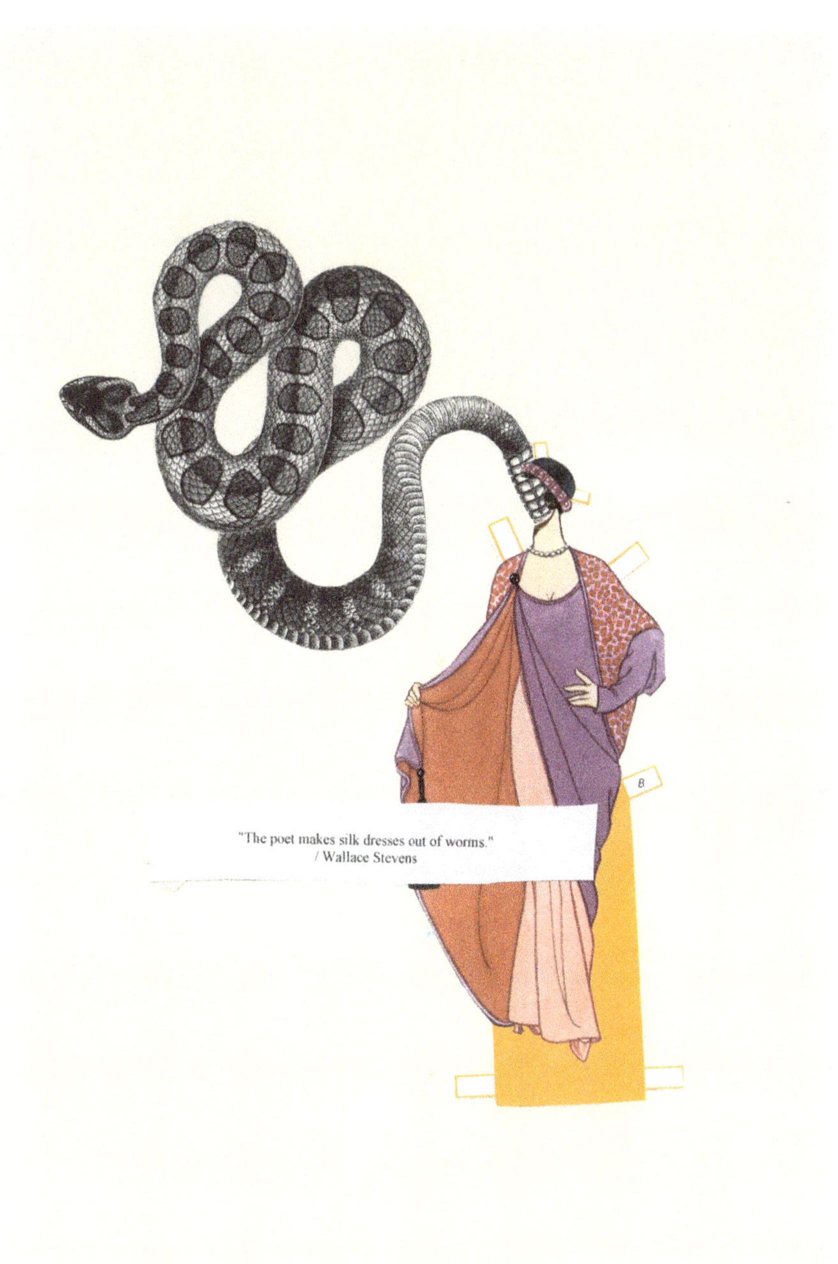

"The poet makes silk dresses out of worms."
/ Wallace Stevens

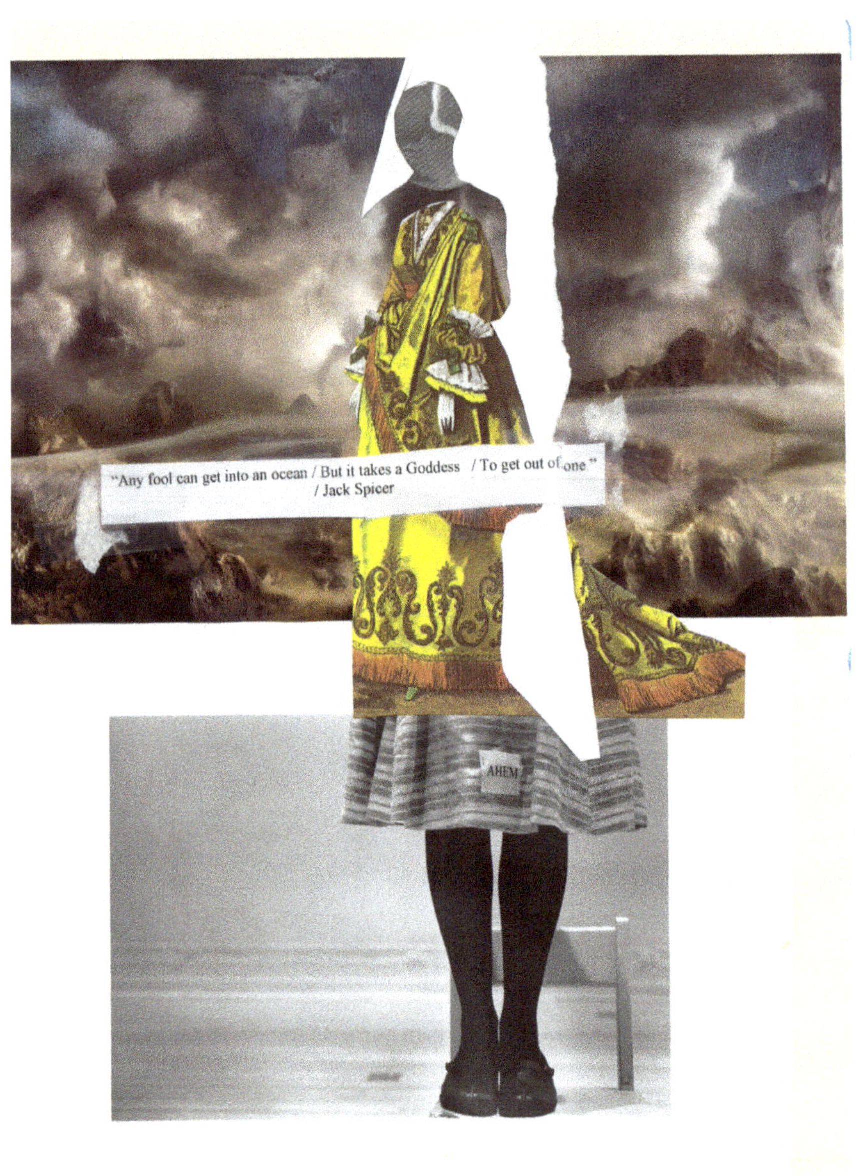

ca. 1900 Worth
Corset

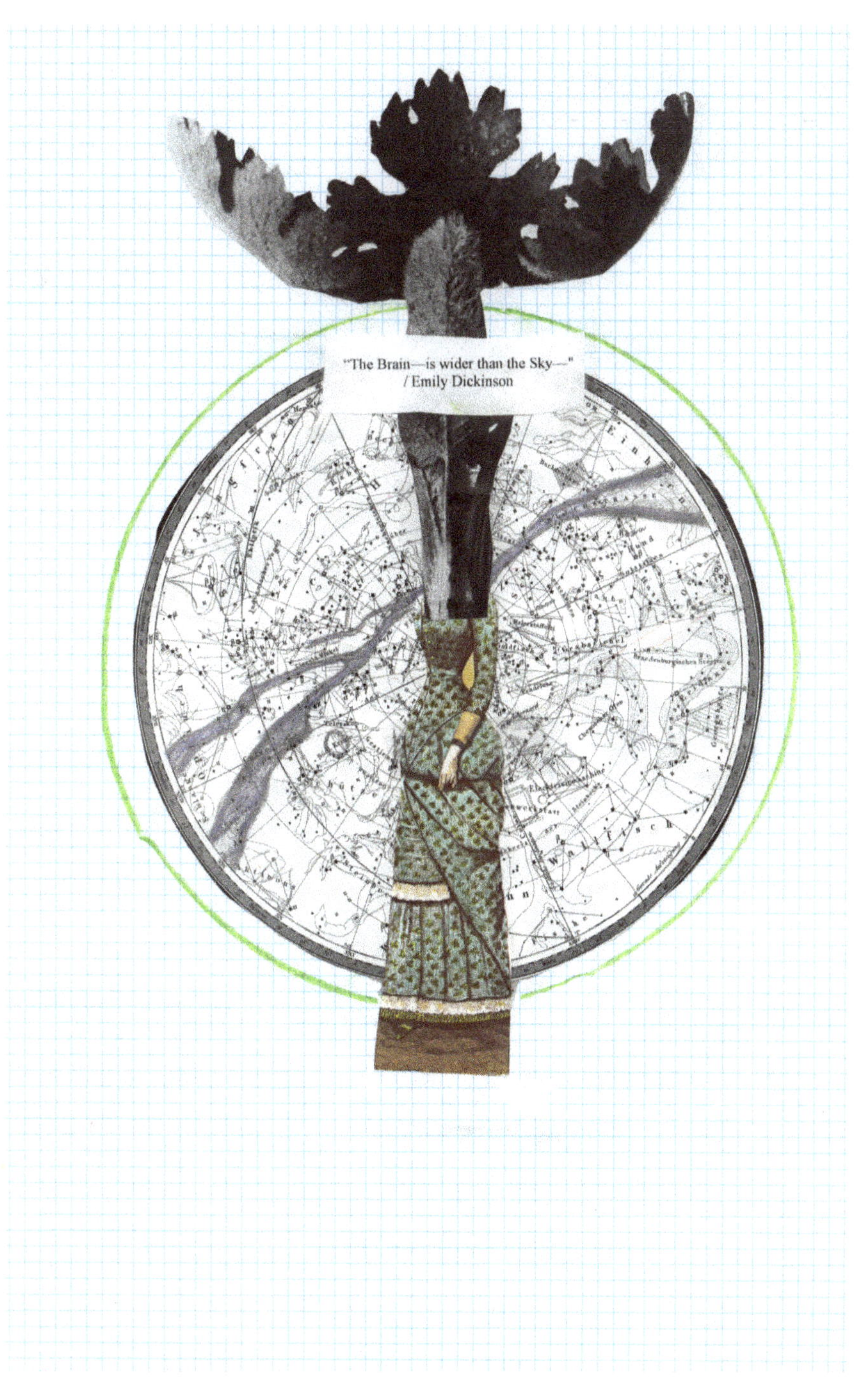
"The Brain—is wider than the Sky—"
/ Emily Dickinson

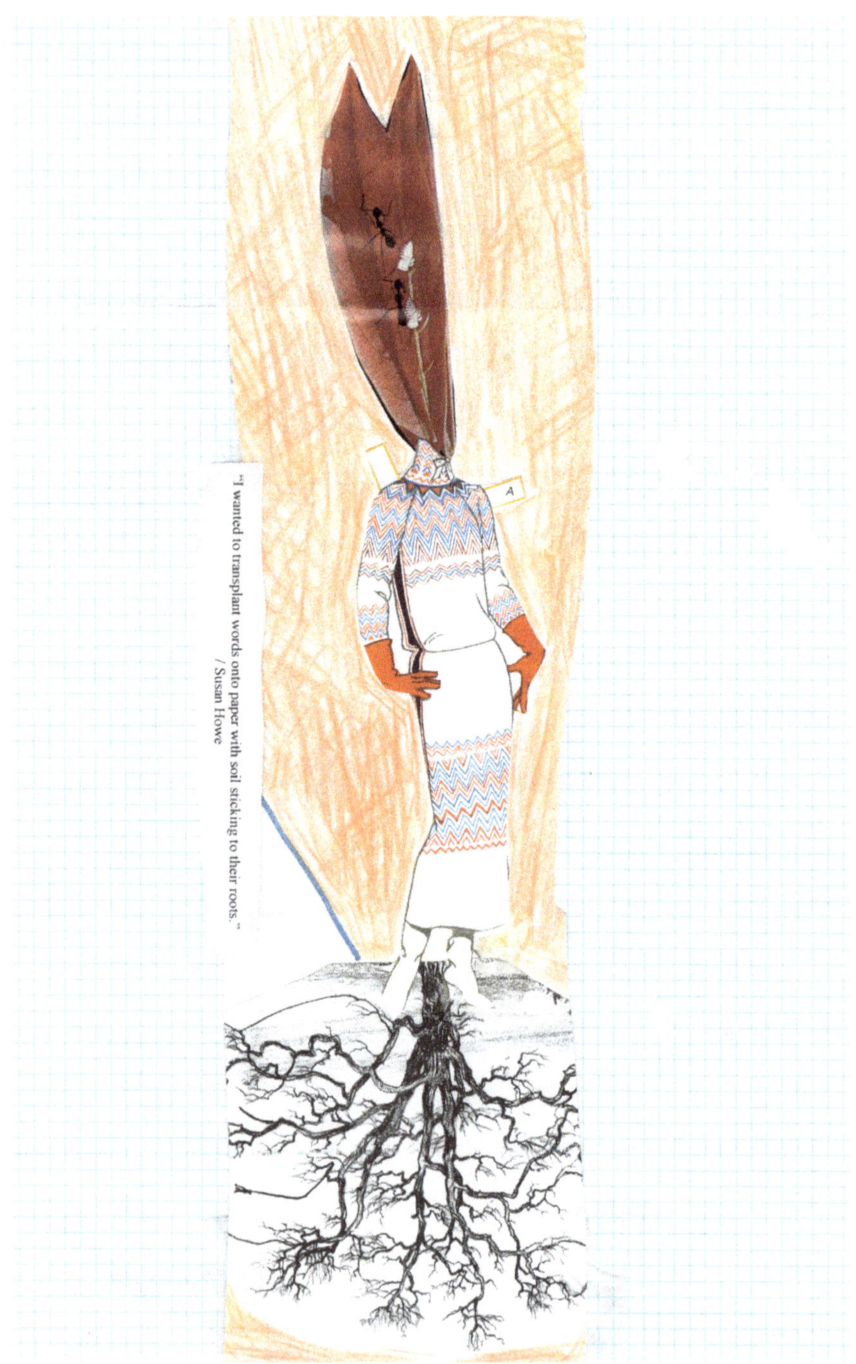

"I wanted to transplant words onto paper with soil sticking to their roots."
/ Susan Howe
A

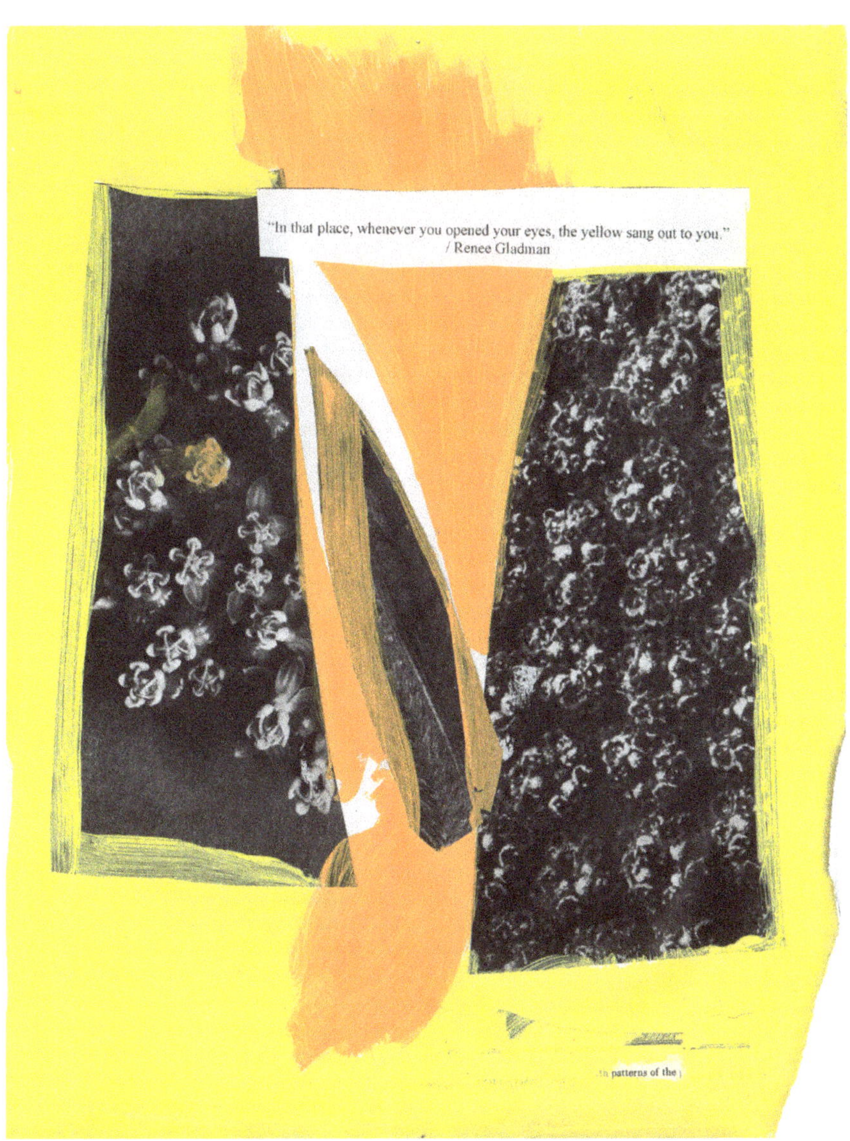

"In that place, whenever you opened your eyes, the yellow sang out to you."
/ Renee Gladman
in patterns of the

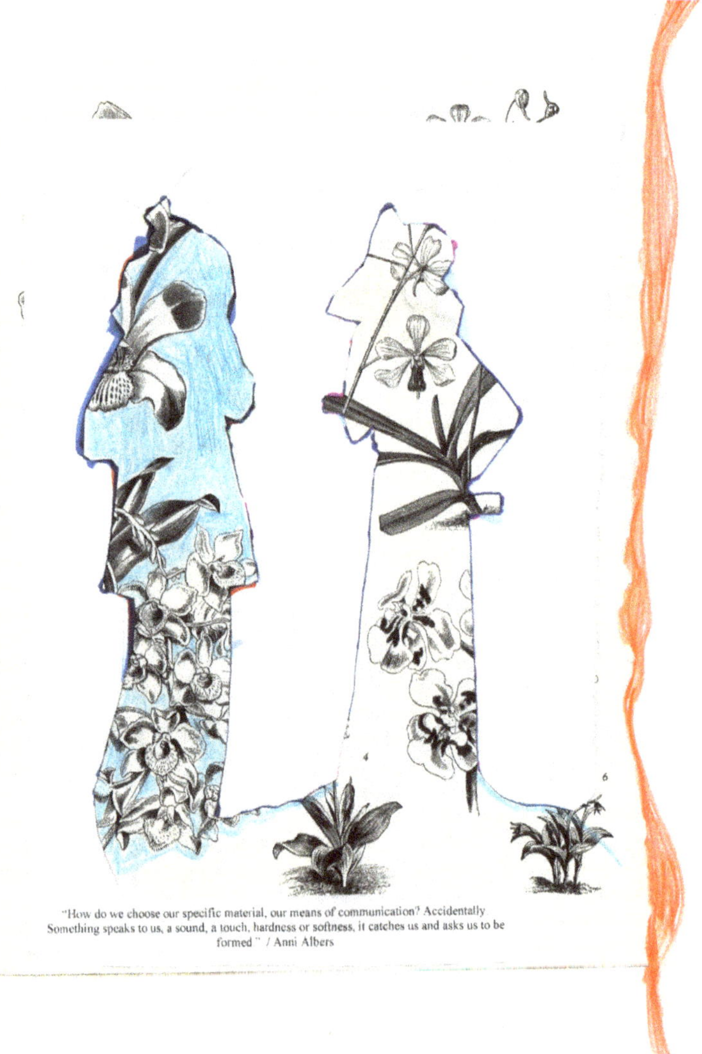

"How do we choose our specific material, our means of communication? Accidentally
Something speaks to us, a sound, a touch, hardness or softness, it catches us and asks us to be
formed." / Anni Albers

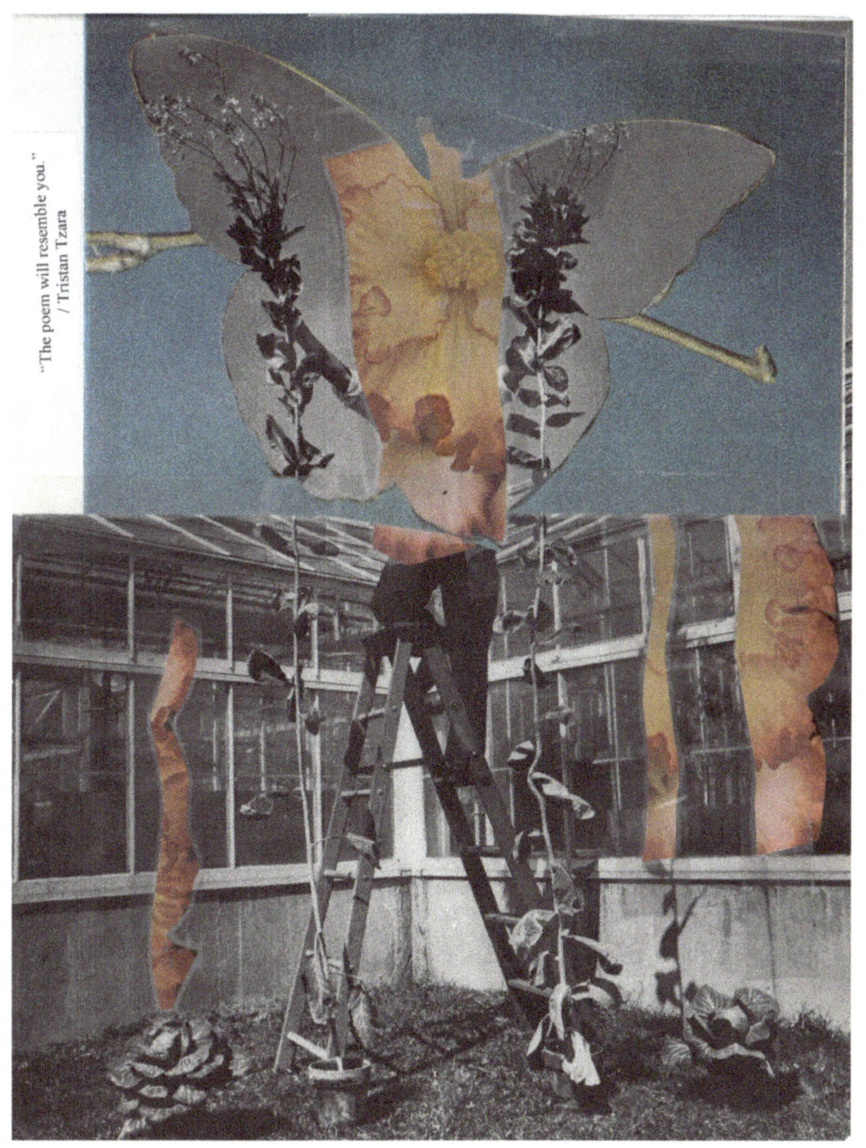

"The poem will resemble you."
/ Tristan Tzara

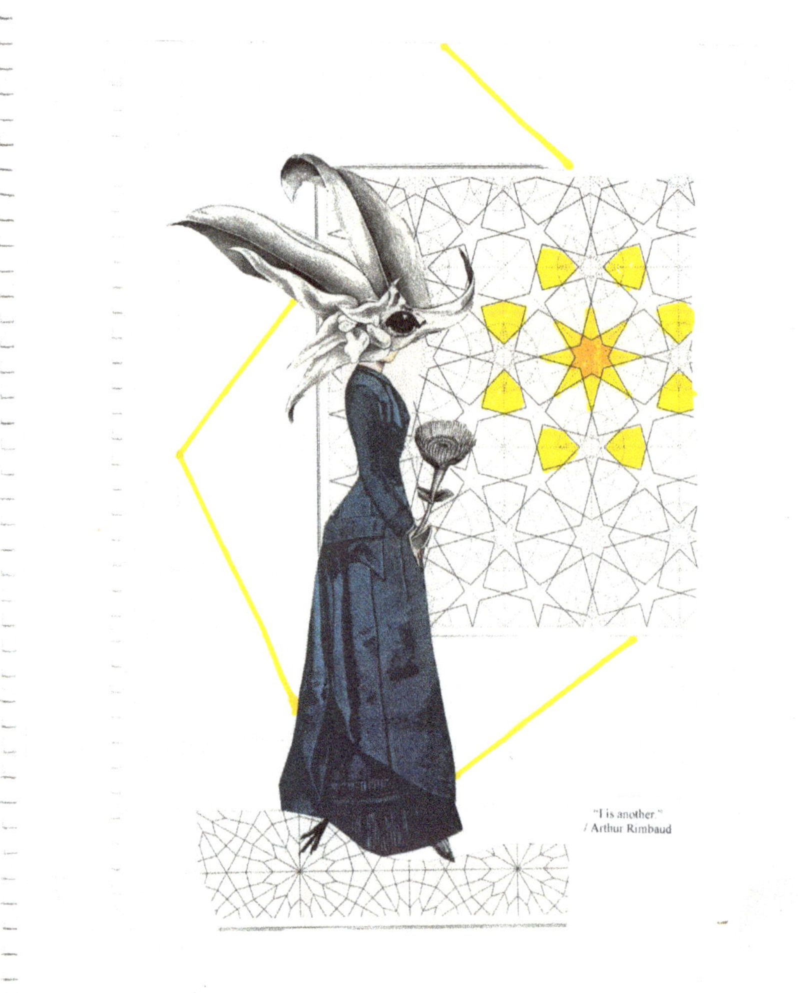
"I is another."
/ Arthur Rimbaud

"Language: forest with all the roots/audible"
/ Hélène Cixous

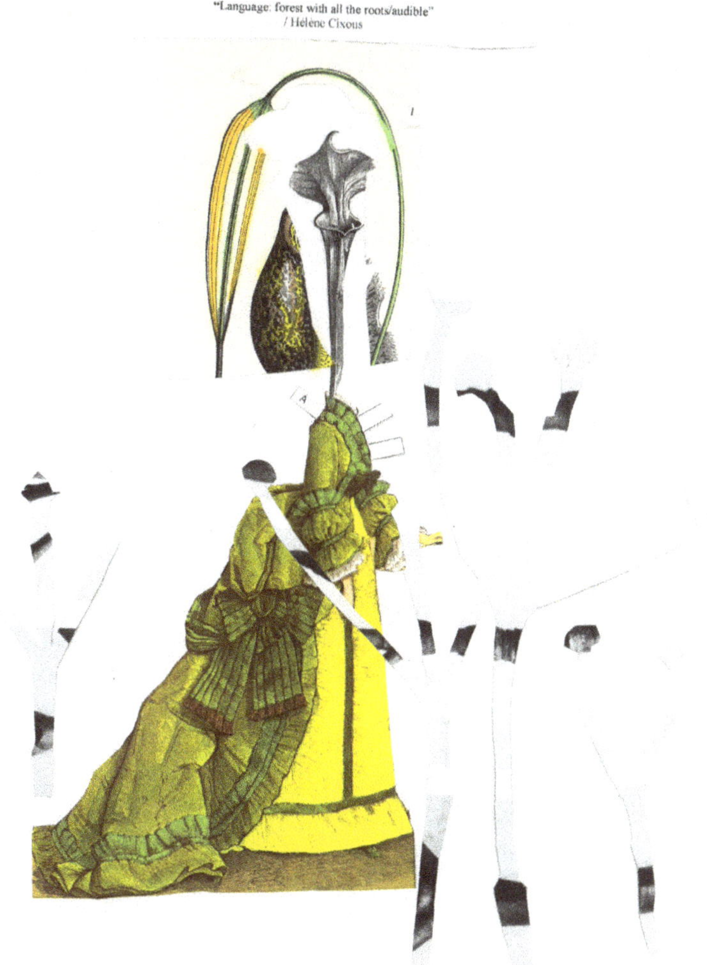

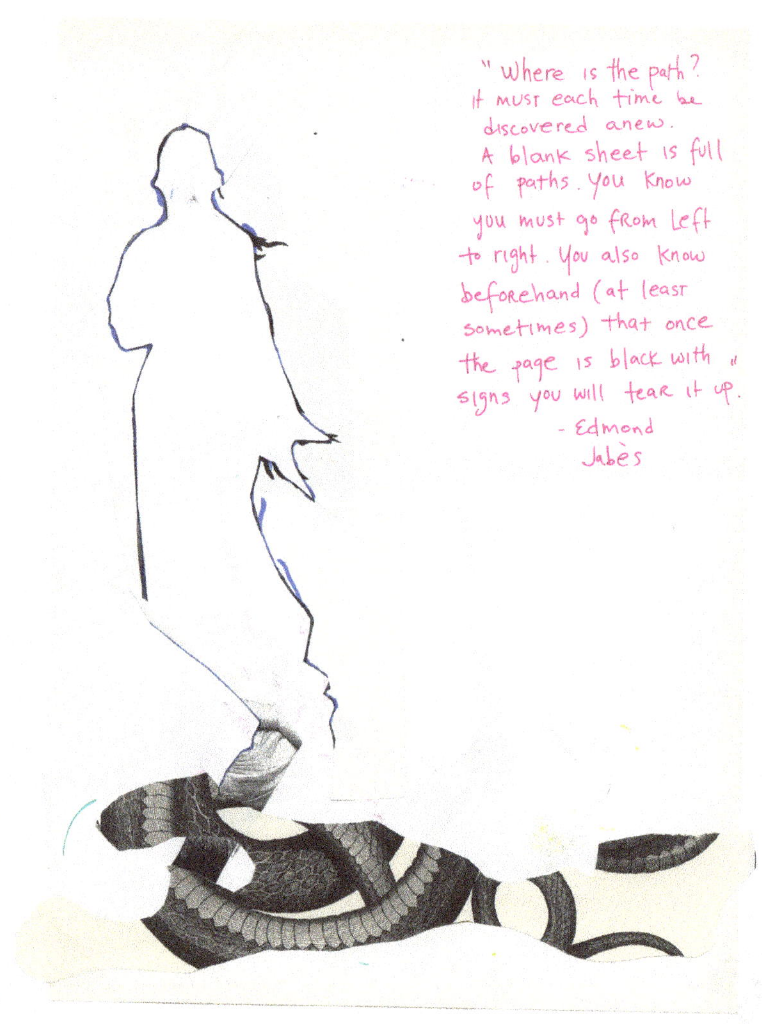

"Where is the path?
It must each time be
discovered anew.
A blank sheet is full
of paths. You know
you must go from left
to right. You also know
beforehand (at least
sometimes) that once
the page is black with
signs you will tear it up."
- Edmond
Jabès

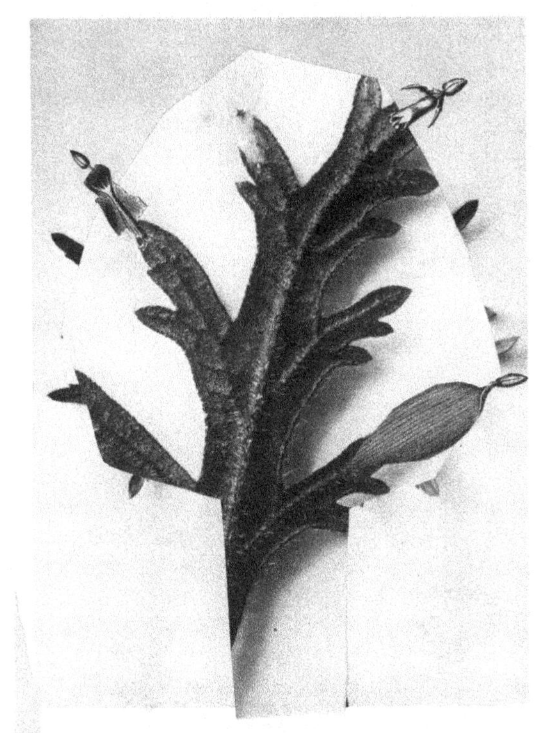

"Within any day there is a hidden dimension both occult and common."
/ Lisa Robertson

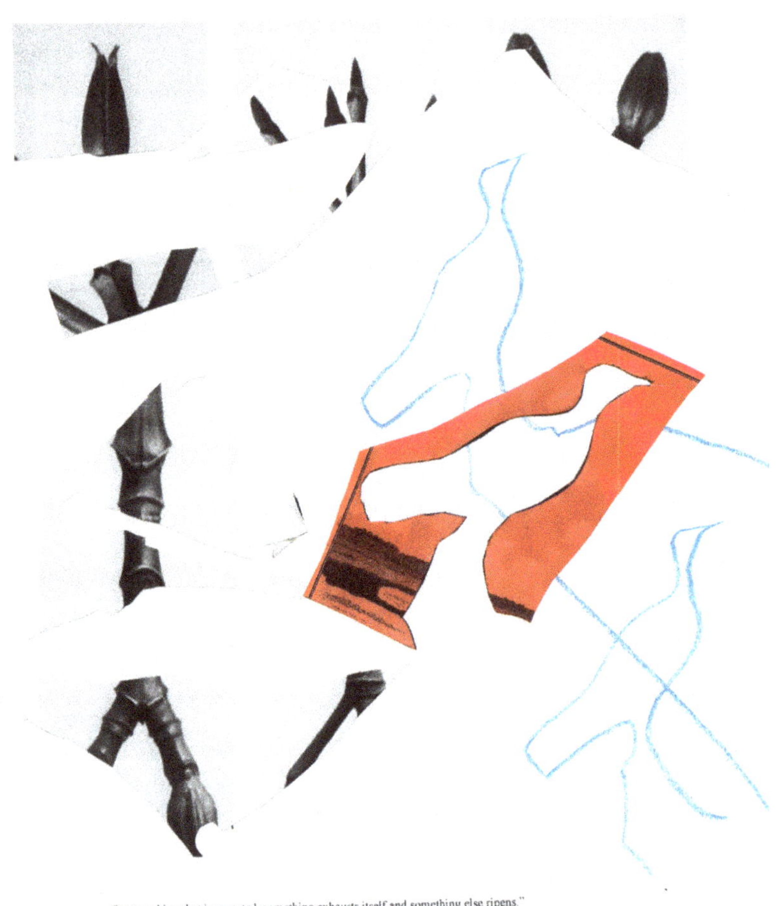

"In everything that is repeated, something exhausts itself and something else ripens."
/ Henri Michaux

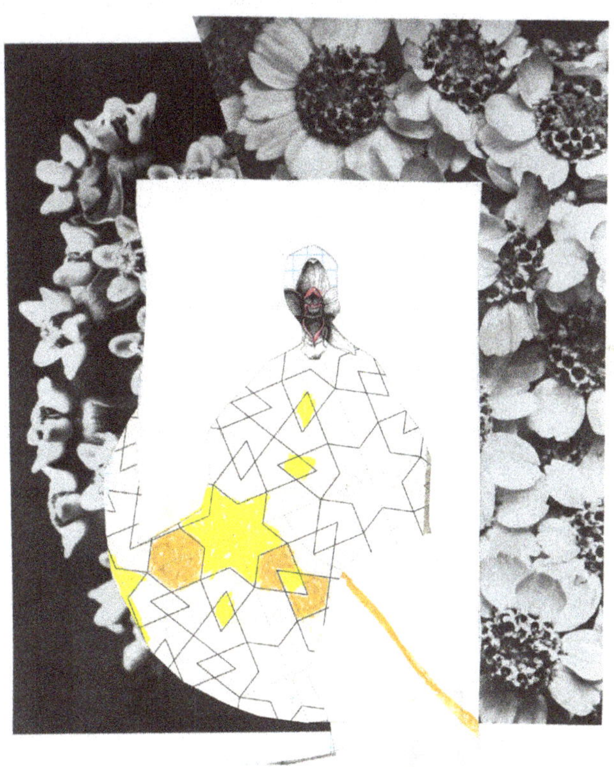

"Art is a wound turned into light."
/ Georges Braque

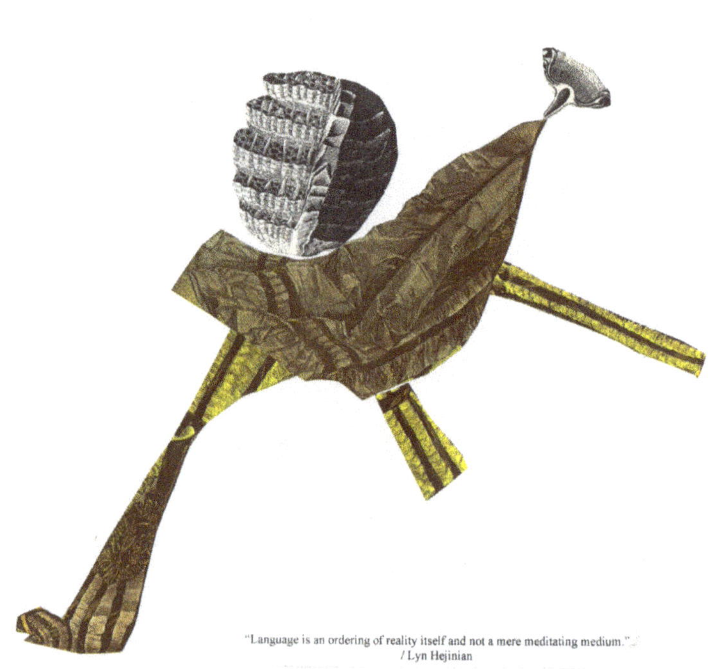

"Language is an ordering of reality itself and not a mere meditating medium."
/ Lyn Hejinian

What Asks Us to Be Formed

What Asks Us to Be Formed

My sister has to come up again.

It's the way repetition works. Something dives down. Another thing comes up for air. To create a hem. Confine. Piece of cloth edging around you. A blank page folding in on the circumference of your body. The subject is one of enclosure and one of breath. To be drowned inside a particular story. The story that is your un-telling.

A sister creates a line. A sister causes divination.

She was born in Budapest in 1979. Given her name by her mother. In 1989 she appears. She was born in Hungary. She was born in the United States. In 1978. She was born in Winfield, IL in the middle of a January blizzard. She was born in April. Flowers bloomed. She was born to a different mother. A mother who gave her her name. She was born, becomes a thread. Becomes entwined to another self, a self overseas. Differently tongued self. Differently threaded.

She began. She emerged as invocation. She became a performance. She became a line.

She became interested in lines as veins. She drew the vein. Intersected life-line.

Held by the palm of the hand like a seedpod held in the mouth. A planet. A plant.

When my sister overdoses on heroin, I go deep into the space of not speaking. When I open my mouth, there is nothing but light seeping out. Always sparks erupting between the gaps of our edges.

The rupture has happened to me.

When I am ten, I come back to Chicago after visiting my mother in California over the summer. My father waits until I'm home to announce that he has remarried and that I have a new sibling, a 10-year-old girl from Hungary, also named Andrea. I can't help but feel utterly replaced, written over, erased. My father's speaking recedes further and further until I feel myself falling through empty space, like I have been dropped from a spaceship into a bottomless void. This is the moment I become a poet.

To reach the interior gesture of grief, I dance the dance of the bees.

I stitch the color of a field inside my intestines. The landscapes that have pierced and embedded themselves in the fabric of my being. From beneath the white sheet of the page, alive in the undercurrent, my mouth gapes and from its hive, a mark, allows the wound to bloom.

When my sister tells me stories of Hungary, before she can speak English, she sounds out in reverberation. I translate the tones and tempos of her body. Her buzzing choreography sending signals to my neural synapses. She speaks inside my body: a méhek és mézük olyan kérdések, amelyek a száj palettáján választ kapnak.

The galeae, labial palp and the glossa a similar defiance. Similar desire for the flight of infinity within the endocrine system.

Two years after my sister's death, my life partner, a poet, will suffer a stroke and I will wonder if he'll ever regain his ability to speak and to read. In this future, I imagine we will no longer be writers. We will move to Indiana, to his parent's house, behind a field of buffalo. We will no longer speak. Our tongues will be intact, but they will be inaccessible, lopped off. We will express ourselves silently, as abstract painters.

My partner is asked to write his name and draws a spiral. He is asked to draw a clock and draws only the right side of its face. "Who is the president?" they ask him multiple times a day, until I ask them to stop. He replaces nearly every noun with the word "communication." "I just want to communicate," he says. A hug is a "communication," a request for water, a "communication." I break out into a burning red rash across my entire body. I do my best to translate his frequencies. I am trained as a Russian spy.

This is something my sister taught me.

How to leave a little space open in the weaving.

*

My first conversation with my sister was one of electricity. We were 10 years old. Both named, Andrea. She and her mother had arrived in Chicago after leaving Hungary in the middle of the night. Unable to speak a common language, we aligned ourselves with static. Communicated by sliding our stockinged feet across the carpeted floor, reaching toward one another, sparks between our edges. We garnered a language of electricity, a volta, sutured ourselves together with this light.

A volta, the threshold, the knot at the center of a bee's flight toward being between.

The bees drone. The bees hum. The bees sting. The bees grieve. The bees sting again, and again.

*

In the ICU, I am unable to speak with any clarity with my partner. I open my mouth and no sound comes out. I am gasping for air. He is flooding. He tries to put marks to the page. I do not understand these sounds he makes. I try to call my sister, but the line is dead.

*

My sister comes up again. Resurfaces to the page. My stubborn sister. My sister from beyond the grave. Always a Queen Bee, my sister.

My sister takes the shape of my cut off tongue. Takes the shape of my name *Andrea Andrea* and calls it her own name Andrea Andrea. Calls it out in a different frequency. Nem a méhek.

*

Velem történt a szakadás. A szakadás velem és a húgommal történt.

A méhek. Az asémikus méhek. A méhek. A méhek. A méhek.

77

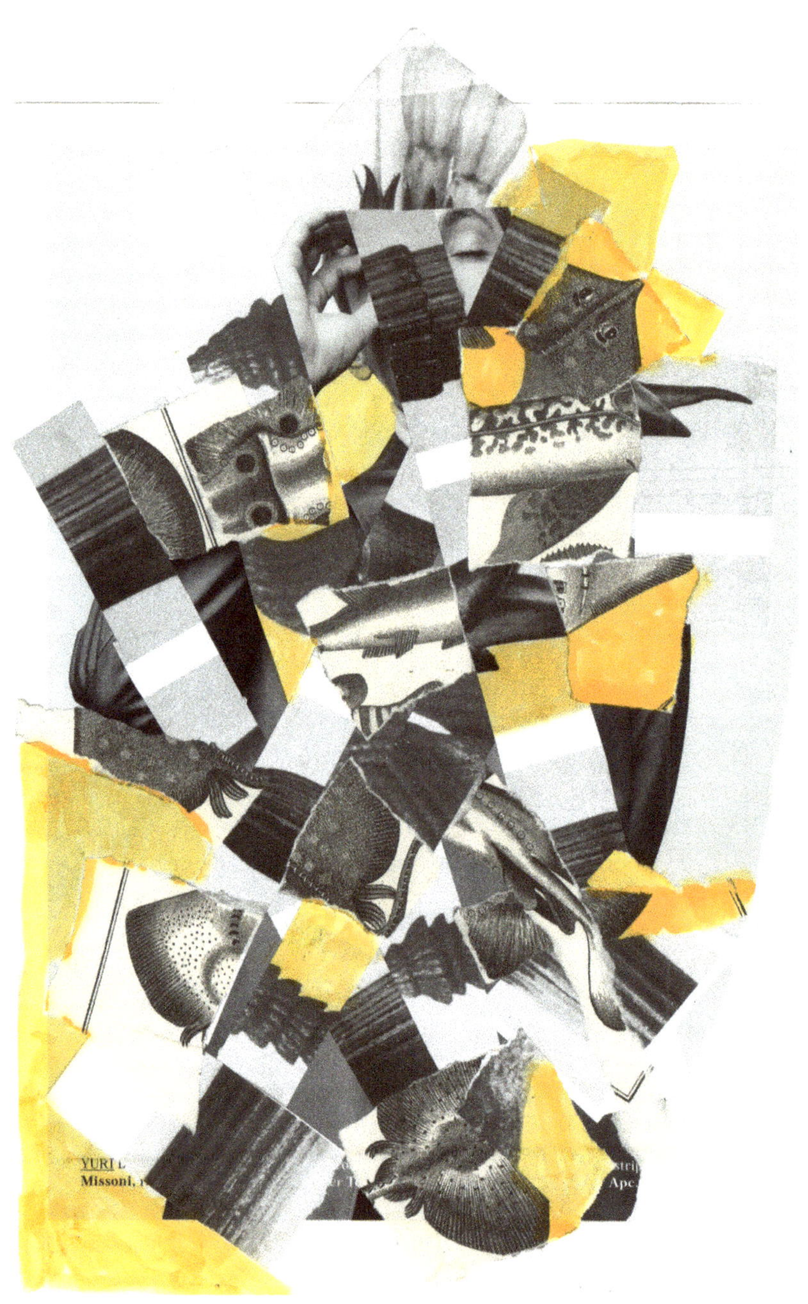

Planchette

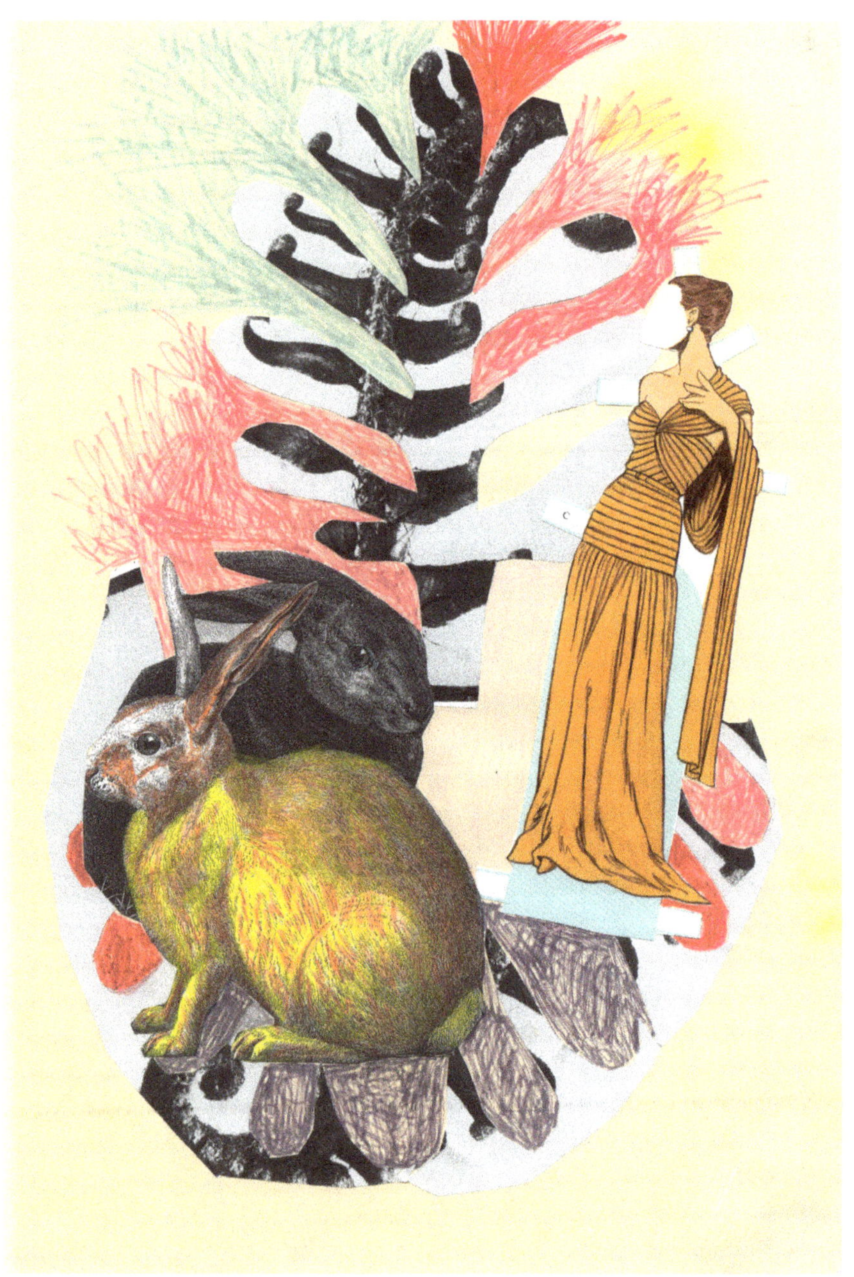

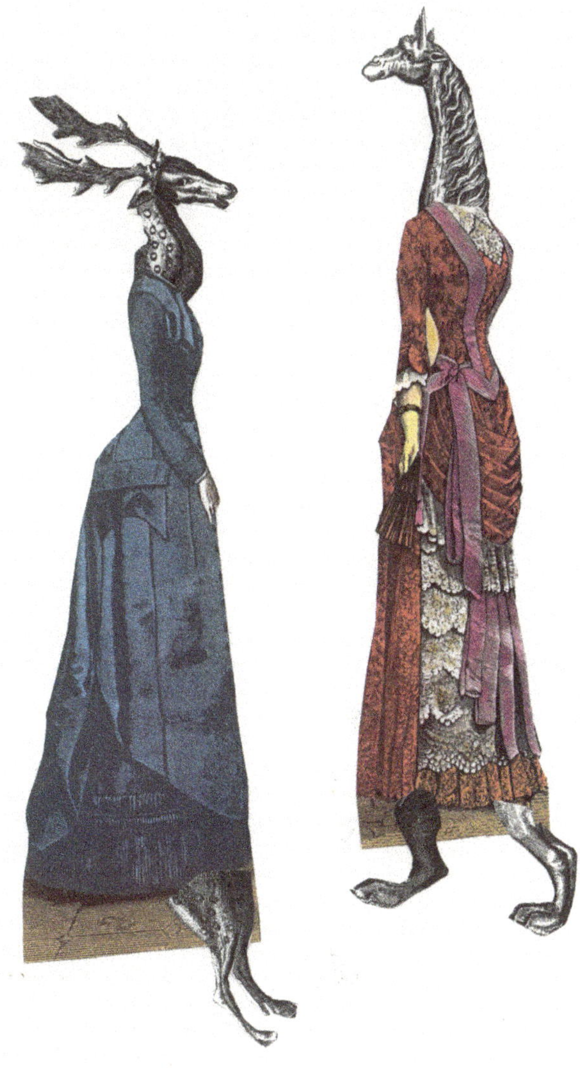

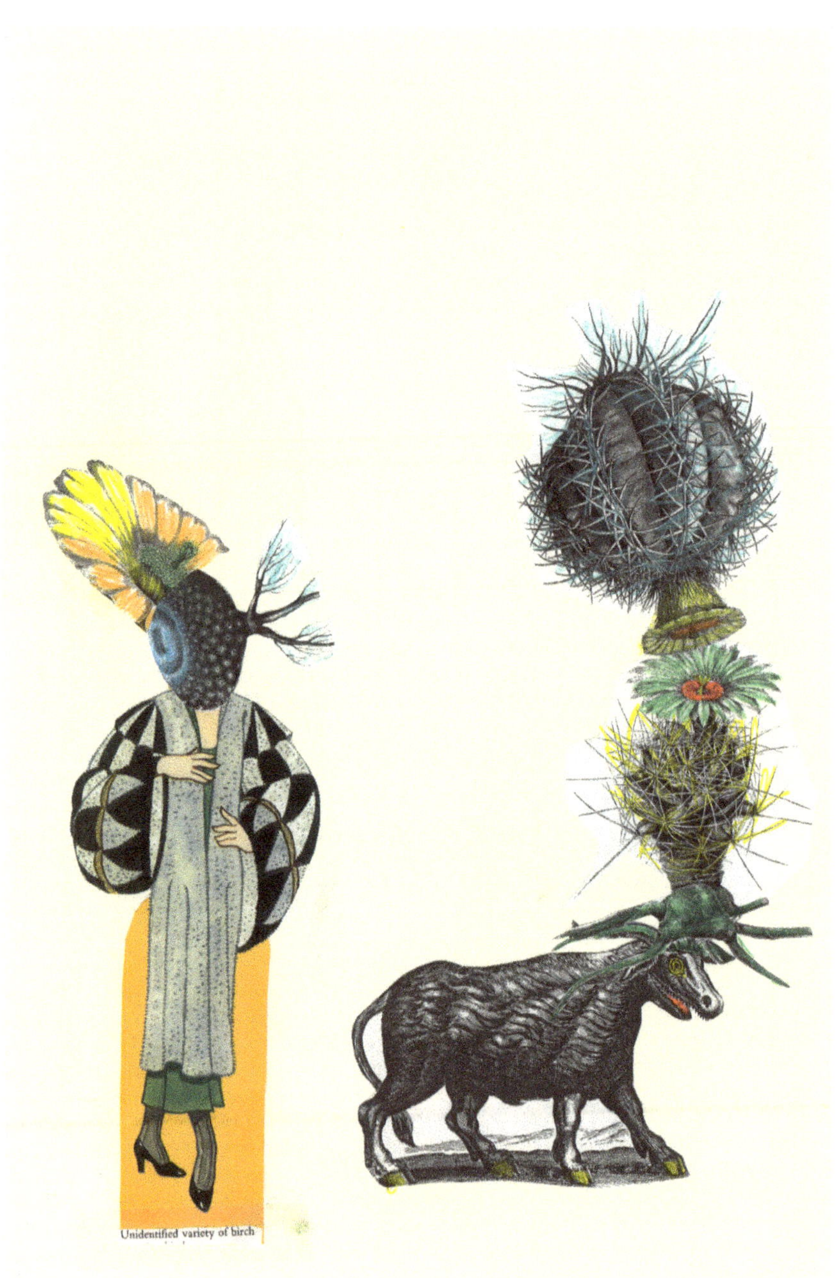

Unidentified variety of birch

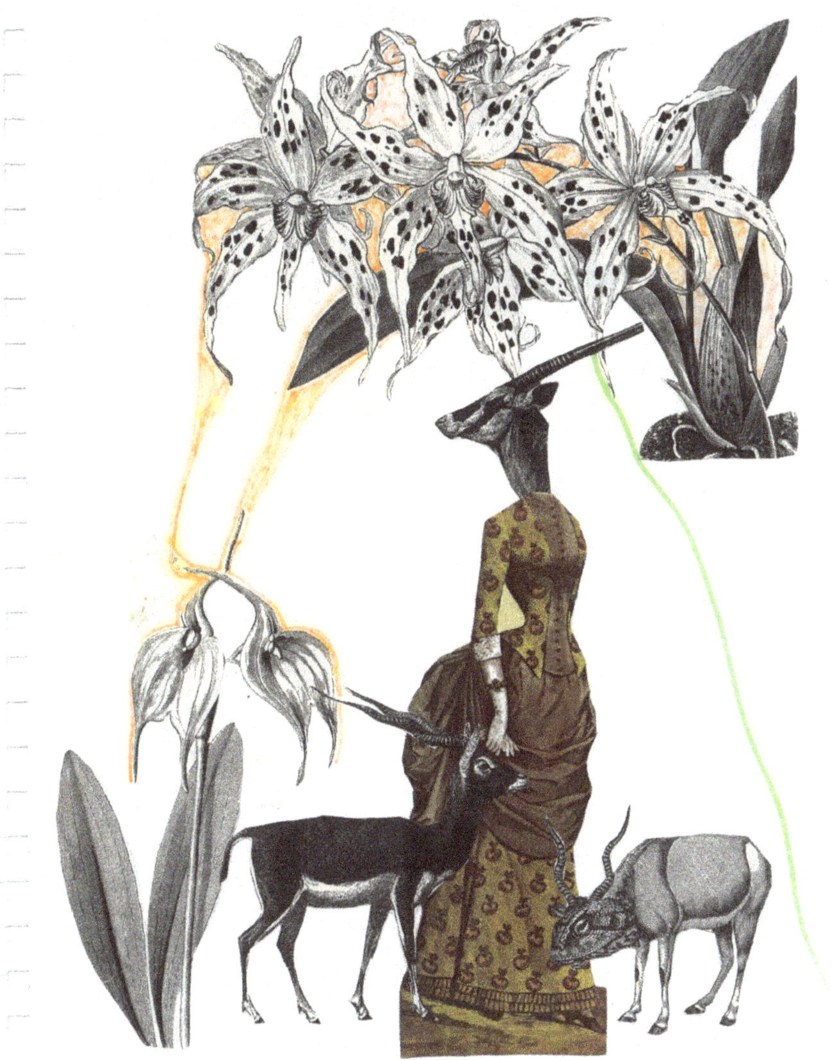

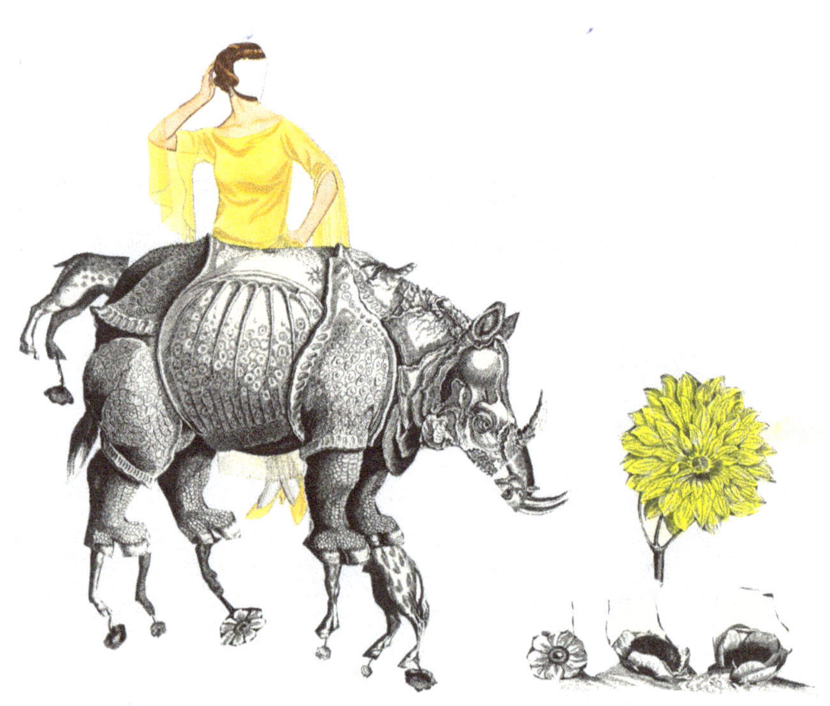

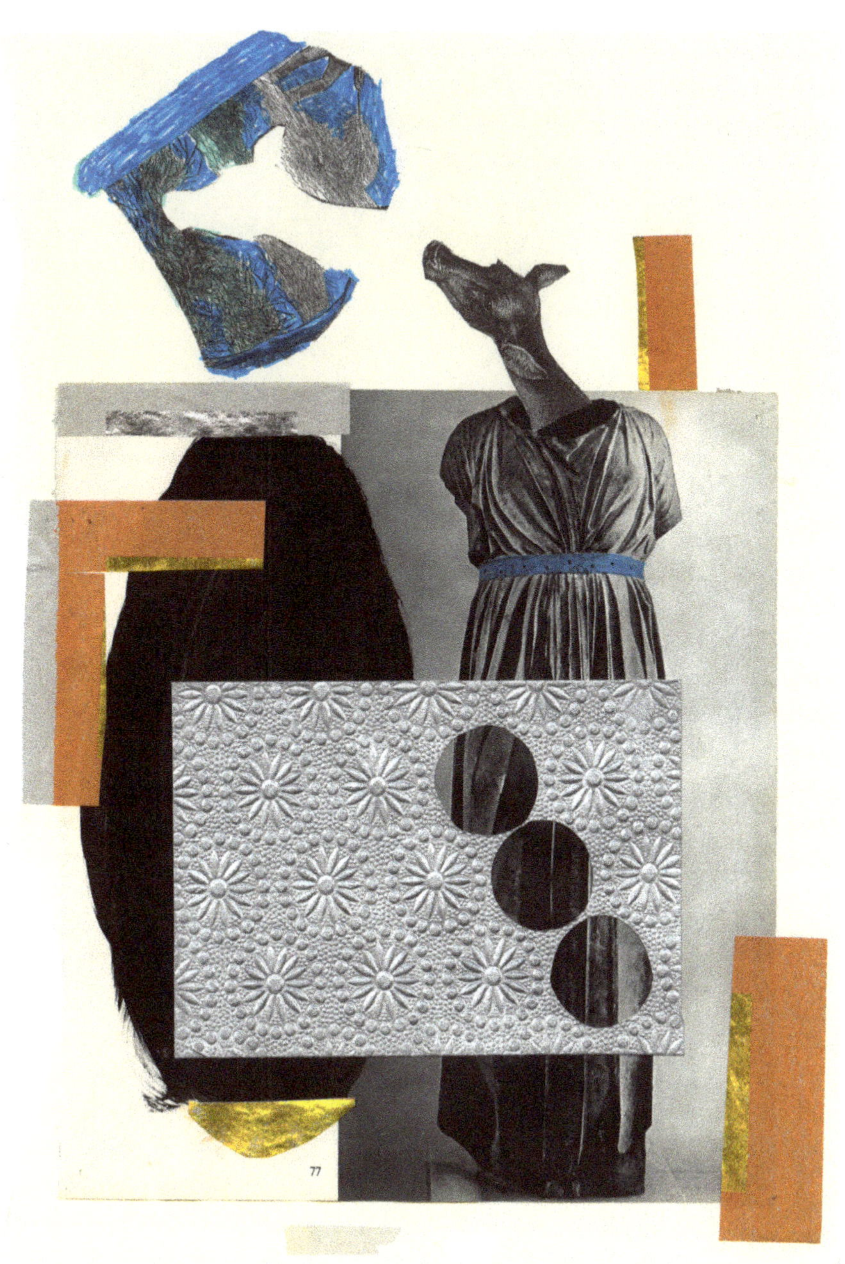
77

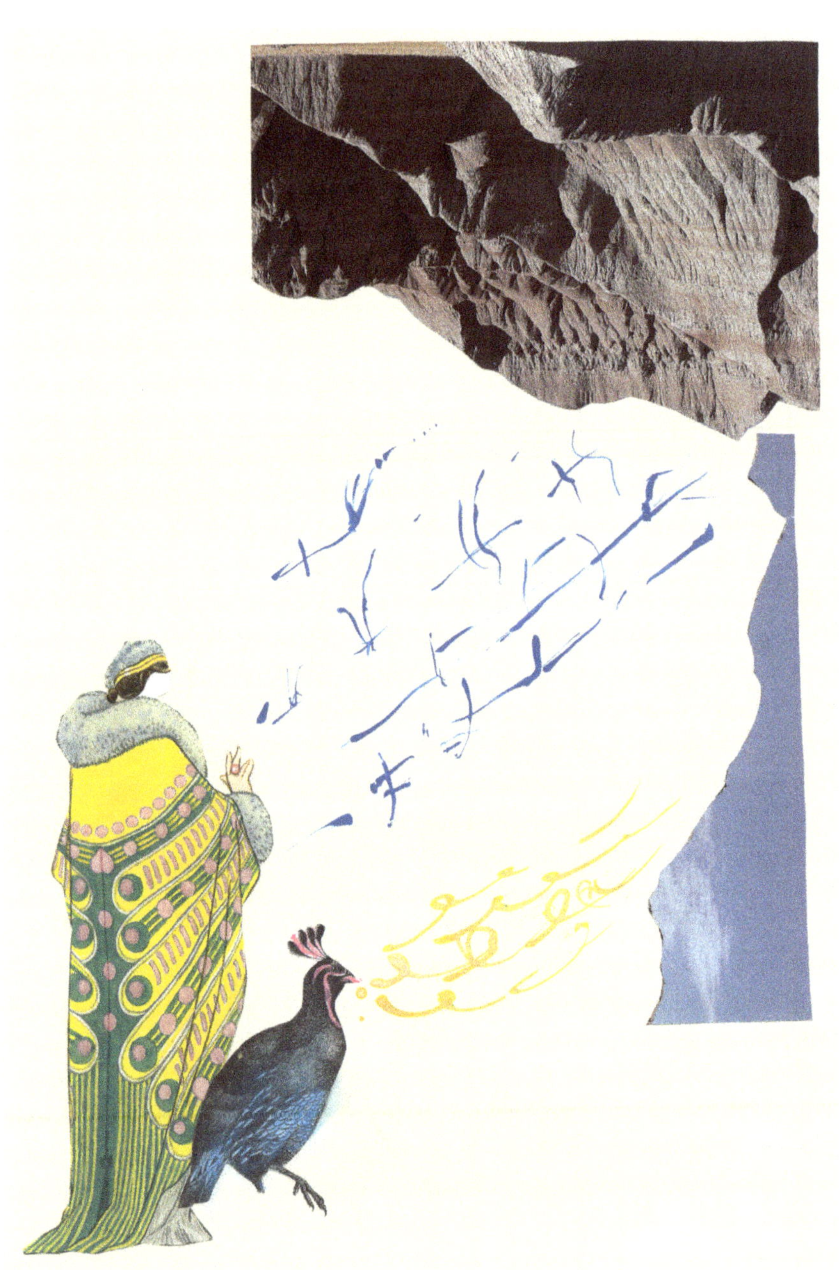

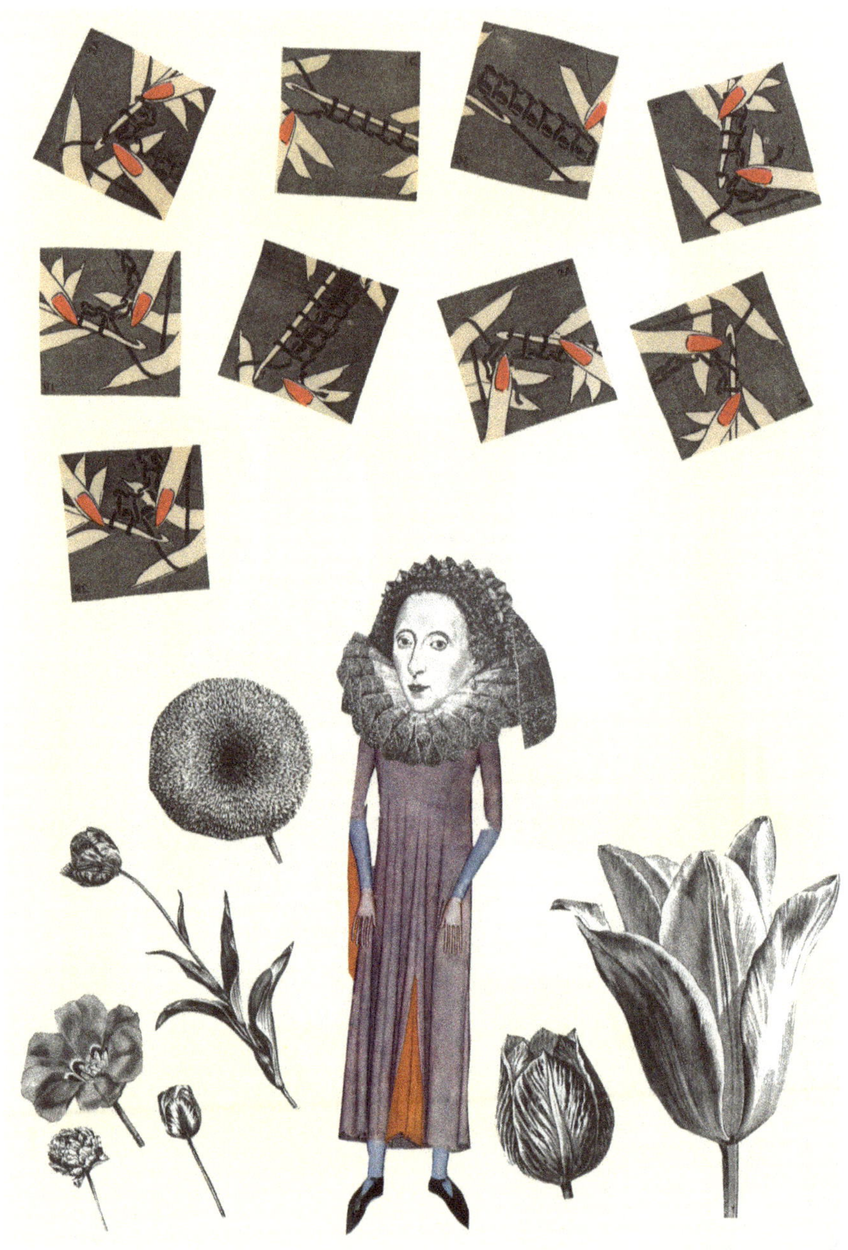

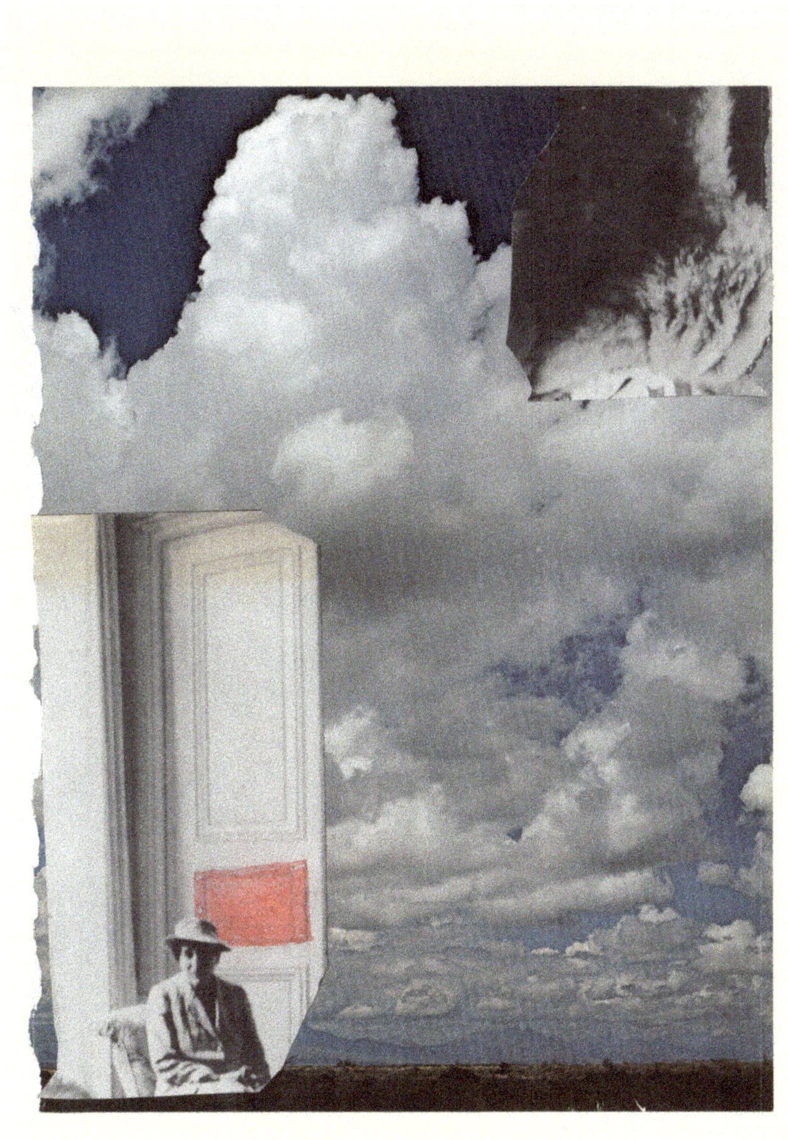

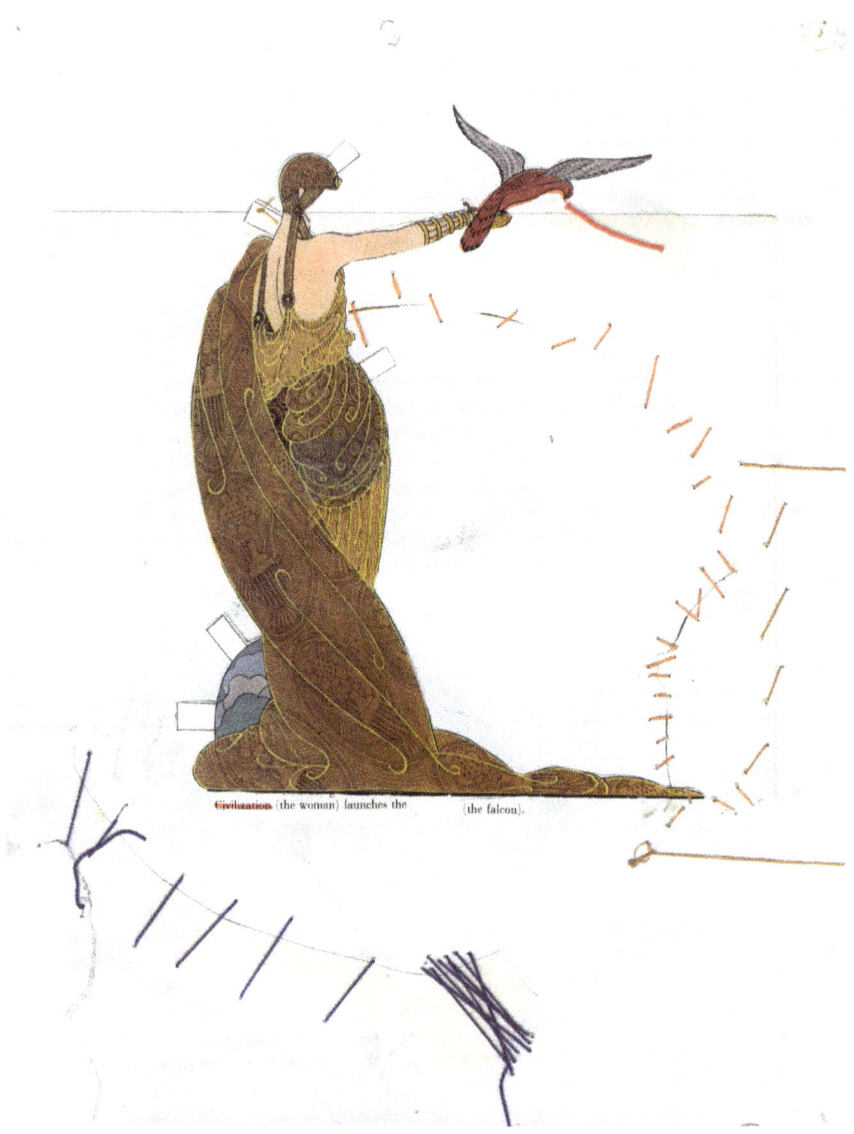

Civilization (the woman) launches the   (the falcon).

Gluing Parts of Different Aphids Together

"Where is the path? It must each time be discovered anew. A blank sheet is full of paths you know you must go from left to right. You also know beforehand (at least sometimes) that once the page is black with signs you will tear it up." —Edmond Jabes

"How do we choose our specific material, our means of communication? Accidentally. Something speaks to us, a sound, a touch, hardness or softness, it catches us and asks us to be formed." —Anni Albers

*

I have always known I was a re-incarnated Dadaist. It began in childhood when I refused to dress as anything other than a sailor. It began at a costume shop I worked at after moving across the country to California when I was 18. It began when I lived in a tool shed next to an abandoned pear orchard and foraged in the forest to survive. It began at poetry readings, where I was too shy to read without wearing a costume (a wig or a mask, in particular). It began with surrealism. With the Russian Futurists. With Kenneth Patchen. With a book arts class. With Henry Darger. It began at a Kinkos in 1996.

I have always felt like I was from a different time period. I am drawn to the dresses of the Victorian Era (less so their literature and rules). I am drawn to the antinomianism of the Puritan Era. The women who gave birth to monsters (stillborns and visions). I have always known I was a witch. I am drawn to the 1920s style of celebration, to the Charleston, to speakeasys, to vaudeville, to the fancy names of drinks. I have always known I embody and channel something from the past.

The poems enclosed in this collection were filed away in folders labeled "scraps." They were written sometime between 1999 and 2024, approximately. They were written by my past selves. They were written by the multitude.

In collage, you don't need ideas; you just need language.

Something arises from within the language.
Something surfaces.   Like compost.

Like the bloom after dead branches are cut away.

To flower.
To open toward new potential.
To garden.   To become
a garden.

I am drawn to the poetic qualities of collage, to the fragmentation, recombination, layering, repetition, pattern, and disruption of pattern. When creating collages, I use the scraps from what I've cut-up to trace/paint new lines/drawings onto the collage. I create in a series, until all the scraps are used.

I use reversals of the images I've cut-out. Cut-outs retain their shape but may gather other images onto their surface that provide interesting textures. For example, a woman with a building on her body. "A woman with a building on her body" is a poem. Sometimes I trace images onto other backgrounds and cut them out. Here I found a tiger made of flowers. "A tiger made of flowers" is another poem.

The poems gathered in this collection collage the past voices of women. Victorian women. Vaudevillian women. Women who are part animal. Women who play accordions and fly on the trapeze. Women out to sea.

Sometimes I make collage paper dolls and perform puppet shows in my lingerie at night. Sometimes I make antlers and wands and papier-mâché butterfly masks and go roller-skating in the park. I am drawn to capes, to bird whistles, to rivers. I climb up trees. I have a certain kind of bravery, a bravado, that is not afraid to leap. I am quiet and reserved, but underneath there is a roar, a cacophony of women, a multi-headed hydra, fierce, but also demure. Medusa is one of my role-models, but in my version of her story, she is the one who cuts off all the heads and recombines them onto animal bodies, fashioning her own mythology. She survives. Sheds her skin and renews. In high school I thought about running away to join the circus. I watched *La Strada* one hundred times. I knew I was Giulietta Masina. I knew I was some version of Hannah Hoch. Instead of having children, I bought dresses. I picked up my scissors. I gathered paper ladies to my side.

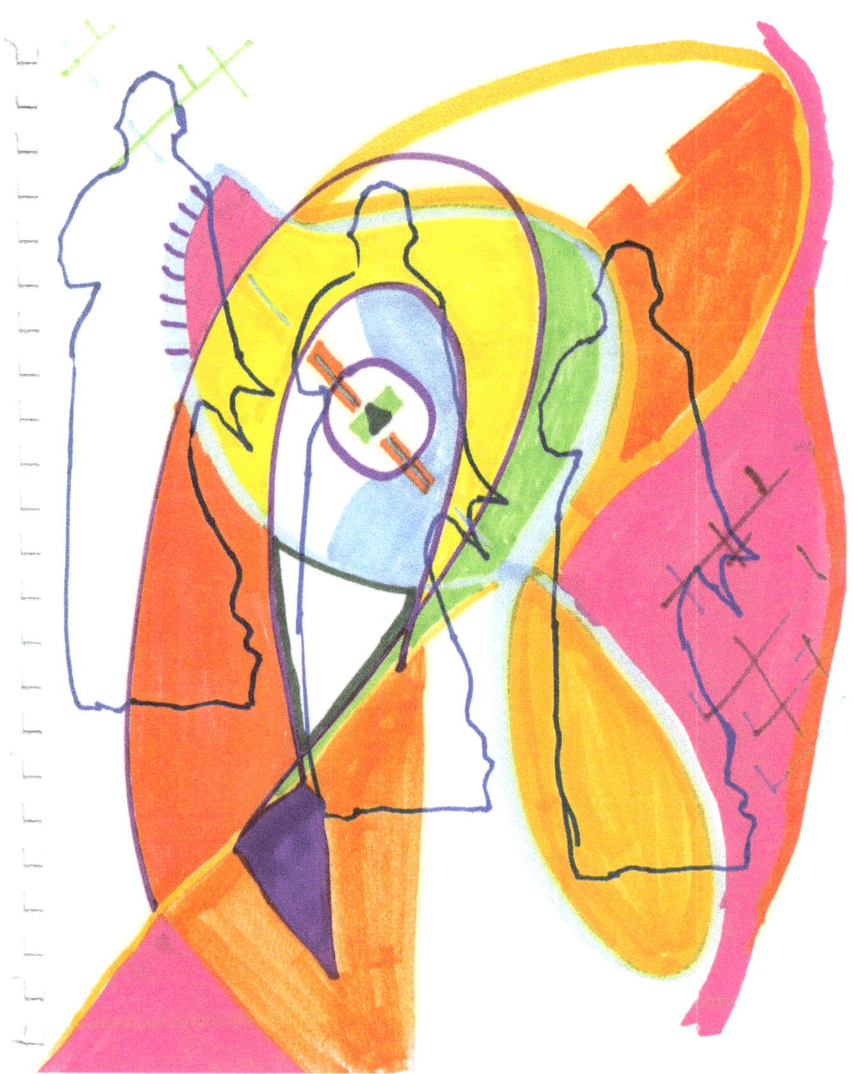

Acknowledgements

Thank you to the editors of the anthology, Sharp Notions for publishing sections of the lyric essay "Becoming Swarm," and to the editors of the literary journals: *Denver Quarterly, Jubilat, New Delta Review, Academy of American Poems*, and *The Rumpus*, for publishing versions of some of these poems. Thank you to *Angel Archers, Hot Pink Mag, Inverted Syntax*, and *Jubilat* for first publishing some of these collages. Thank you, *CLASH Books* for making space for art and writing to intermingle!

About the Author

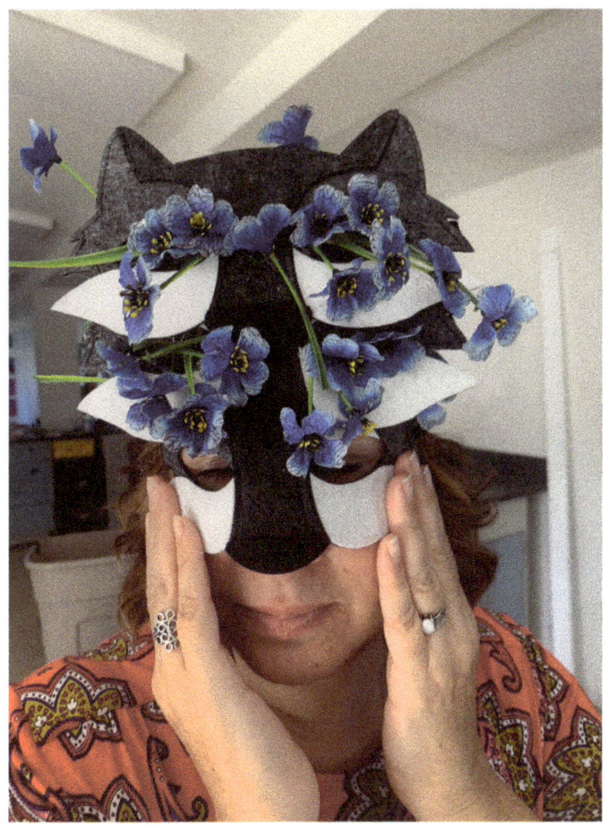

Andrea Rexilius is the author of: *Sister Urn* (Sidebrow, 2019), *New Organism: Essais* (Letter Machine, 2014), *Half of What They Carried Flew Away* (Letter Machine, 2012), and *To Be Human Is To Be A Conversation* (Rescue Press, 2011), as well as editor of the anthologies: *We Can See into Another Place: Mile-High Writers on Social Justice* (Bower House/The Bookies, 2024) and *The Braided River: Activist Rhizome* (Essay Press, 2015). Andrea is the Program Director for Regis University's Mile-High MFA in Creative Writing. She also teaches in the Poetry Collective at Lighthouse Writers Workshop in Denver, Colorado.

Also by CLASH Books

I MADE AN ACCIDENT
Kevin Sampsell

SEPARATION ANXIETY
Janice Lee

WAR IS NOT MY MOTHER
Vi Khi Nao

THE SORROW FESTIVAL
Erin Salughter

WITCH HUNT & BLACK CLOUD
Juliet Escoria

ALMANAC OF USELESS TALENTS
Michael Chang

AN EXHALATION OF DEAD THINGS
Savannah Slone

SAD SEXY CATHOLIC
Lauren Milici

VHS
Chris Campanioni